People Skills

Titles in the *Macmillan Modern Office* Series

Business Administration III Pack	McFetridge
Count on Confidence: The Way in to Personal Effectiveness	Chisholm
Elementary Exercises in Word Processing – Student's Book, Teacher's Book	Brown & Tiffney
English Language Skills	Hughes
Integrated Assignments in Secretarial, Office and Business Procedures Pack	McFetridge
Intermediate Exercises in Word Processing – Student's Book, Teacher's Book	Brown & Tiffney
Quickly into QWERTY	Hughes
Self Presentation Skills	Hughes & Weller
Starting in the Office Pack	Barnes

Easily into . . .

dBase III Plus (Exercise disks available)	Gosling
Desk Top Publishing	Gosling
DisplayWrite 4	Gosling
DOS (Exercise disks available)	Gosling
LocoScript for the Amstrad PCW	Rogers
Lotus 1–2–3	Gilligan
MultiMate Advantage II	Gosling
MultiMate Advantage II Advanced	Gosling
WordStar	Simons
WordStar 1512	Gosling
WordStar 2000 Release 2	Simons
WordStar 2000 Advanced	Simons
WordStar 2000 Release 3	Simons

Macmillan Modern Office

Series Editor: Christine Simons

PEOPLE SKILLS
Building Business Relationships

Vera Hughes

MACMILLAN

First published 1992 by
MACMILLAN EDUCATION LTD
Houndmills, Basingstoke, Hampshire RG21 2XS
and London
Companies and representatives
throughout the world

ISBN 0–333–55715–8

A catalogue record for this book is available
from the British Library.

Typeset by Wearside Tradespools, Boldon, Tyne and Wear

Printed in Hong Kong

10	9	8	7	6	5	4	3	2	1
01	00	99	98	97	96	95	94	93	92

☐ Contents

Acknowledgements

As always, I am most grateful to my partner, David Weller, for his encouragement and patience while the book was being written, and for his expertise in keying it in.

I also acknowledge, with thanks, all the people skills ideas I have learnt through working with the Training and Motivation Department of Purchasepoint.

☐ Introduction

 ## Is this book for you?

Do you have to deal with people at work? Are you starting out in
working life? Are you part of a team or a team leader? Would you prefer
to work in a positive rather than a negative atmosphere?

If you want to build and improve your business relationships, this
book **is** for you.

 ## What will you learn from this book?

This book will help you to deal with all sorts of people in the work
environment and to make sure you tackle each situation in the right
way.

You will learn how to listen to people, how to respond and how to
get the best out of the most difficult situations, on the telephone and
face-to-face. Many of the exercises or practice sessions will cover
Elements, or in some cases entire Units, in your NVQ (National
Vocational Qualification) competences.

There are no set rules about how to deal with people, because
people are people, and each person is different, but there are guidelines
and suggestions you can use. Occasional self-assessment exercises
encourage you to analyse how you think and behave, and how this
affects the people you work with.

 ## How does it work?

It works in two ways. You can work through it from beginning to end to
help you build your business relationships in the different situations
you are likely to find yourself in.

You can use it to help you deal with specific situations – 'How to say no' for example, or when you have to delegate a task to someone else.

Like the other two books in this series *English Language Skills* and *Self Presentation Skills*, use it in the way most suitable for you.

At the beginning of each chapter you will find a list of the main points covered – these are a repeat of the points in the Contents table, which you can use to look for general headings. If you want to study a very specific situation which you cannot find in the Contents table (Open Learning, for example) look in the Index.

Each chapter has exercises to do as you work through it, or a practice session at the end, or sometimes both. Each chapter also has a checklist of points to remember.

 ## Situations covered in the book

Chapter 1 is a very general chapter about people and what makes them tick. It introduces the idea of external customers (people you deal with outside your company or organisation) and internal customers (the people you work with). Read this chapter as a basis for the rest of the book. The external/internal theme is used all the way through.

The next two chapters concentrate on the development of your own skills in listening, responding, questioning, greeting, parting and using positive body language – all skills you will need as you cope with various people situations. These are followed by four chapters on the different tricky situations you might come across.

Chapters 8 and 9 concentrate on your skills in working with people as part of a team or through other people if you are a team leader – even if your team is only two people, you and one other. This self-improvement theme is carried through into a chapter on how to get the best out of development opportunities such as appraisals, assessments, self-study, training courses and work experience.

The last two chapters are about opportunities for giving quality service in your job, whatever it is. They encourage you to think creatively, to avoid getting stuck in a rut and to put your ideas into practice without upsetting other people.

You spend a large part of your life at work. This book will help you develop your people skills; it will help you build the business relationships which often make all the difference between work which you passively accept and work which you actively enjoy.

1 Everyone Deals with People

In this chapter:
- Are you a people person?
- What makes a person?
- The people you deal with
  - external customers
  - internal customers
- What people need from you

 Are you a people person?

Well, are you? Do people say of you: 'so and so is good to work with, or to work for'? Does it matter?

The sub-title of this book is 'Building Business Relationships' and in your working life, as well as in your private life, it is important that people want and are able to work with or for you. Wherever you work, you are part of a team; good teamwork is impossible if the members of that team are unable to communicate with each other because they cannot get on. This does not mean that they have to like each other, but they need to work in harmony to complete the tasks they are setting out to achieve.

Some people are naturally 'people people'; others have to work at it. Nearly everyone has some weaknesses in the way they deal with others. Do this quiz to discover whether you are a people person at this stage in your life. You must be honest in the answers you give, or it will not work.

To each of the following questions, answer by ticking the Yes (Y), No (N) or Maybe (M) column. Write the answers down quickly, without thinking too deeply about them.

1

2

	Quiz	Y	N	M
1	Do you usually do most of the talking?			
2	Do you go out of your way to make people like you?			
3	Do you lose your temper easily?			
4	Do you enjoy going to school, college or work?			
5	Do you avoid people whose manners you don't like?			
6	If you are in trouble, do you ask for help?			
7	Can you keep your mouth shut and listen to others?			
8	Are you easily discouraged?			
9	Do people often frighten you?			
10	Are you as quick to express appreciation as to find fault?			
11	Do you let a tone of exasperation, boredom or sarcasm creep into your voice?			
12	Do you let other people go first?			
13	Are you often late?			
14	Do you look at people when they are talking to you?			

You should have ticked Y, N or M against each question. Now score your answers, as follows:
- For every M score 2
- For question 1 score 1 for Y and 3 for N
  For question 2 score 1 for Y and 3 for N
  For question 3 score 1 for Y and 3 for N
  For question 4 score 3 for Y and 1 for N
  For question 5 score 1 for Y and 3 for N
  For question 6 score 3 for Y and 1 for N
  For question 7 score 3 for Y and 1 for N
  For question 8 score 1 for Y and 3 for N
  For question 9 score 1 for Y and 3 for N
  For question 10 score 3 for Y and 1 for N
  For question 11 score 1 for Y and 3 for N
  For question 12 score 3 for Y and 1 for N
  For question 13 score 1 for Y and 3 for N
  For question 14 score 3 for Y and 1 for N

Now add up your score. Out of 42 if you got 35+ you are probably a real people person. 25–35 you are quite good at working with people. 15–25 you are not bad, but you need to work at it. Under 15 HELP!

This is not a scientifically-based quiz, but a bit of fun. If you try to analyse your answers, it will tell you a little bit about the sort of person you are when it comes to working with others, and it will show you the areas you need to work at. Check through each question again, and think about how you scored and what it means about you.

Question 1 – Do you usually do most of the talking?
If you talk a lot, it means you are probably not a very good listener, and you need to listen well to be a good communicator.

Question 2 – Do you go out of your way to make people like you?
You might be surprised at the scoring here but people who go out of their way to make others like them can be ingratiating and sometimes smarmy. It is not necessary to like the people you work with, but of course it helps. Most people like to be liked, but at work it is not even necessary for other people to like you.

Question 3 – Do you lose your temper easily?
If you do, it shows a lack of maturity and self-control.

Question 4 – Do you enjoy going to school, college or work?
It could be that you find school, college or work very boring, but if you are a people person at least you will enjoy working with the people around you, or learning from them. Life is sometimes as boring as you make it.

Question 5 – Do you avoid people whose manners you don't like?
It is very understandable that people do avoid people whose manners they don't like, but if you are a real people person you will try to overlook their bad manners and show by the way you work how much better it is to have good manners.

Question 6 – If you are in trouble, do you ask for help?
Many people think it is a weakness to ask for help, but in fact it is a strength, because it shows you have enough confidence in yourself and others to be able to acknowledge that you do not know something and they do.

Question 7 – Can you keep your mouth shut, and listen to others?
This goes with question 1 of course, but when you listen, do you listen well and actively?

4

Question 8 – Are you easily discouraged?
If you give up easily, do not see a job through to the end or cannot be bothered to find mistakes when you know you have made them, people will get fed up with you and think you are not a good person to work with.

Question 9 – Do people often frighten you?
It is easy to be frightened when you first start work because they seem to know so much more, or they assume you should be able to do things, and shout at you. If you can put yourself in their shoes and remember that they were new once, you will probably not feel so frightened of them. If they shout, they have lost control anyway. A good people person will understand this.

Question 10 – Are you as quick to express appreciation as to find fault?
People often find it difficult to see what is well done and **tell** the other person so, but good people people make a practice of doing this.

Question 11 – Do you let a tone of exasperation, boredom or sarcasm creep into your voice?
If you do, you are putting the other person down – not the act of a good people person.

Question 12 – Do you let other people go first?
Good manners demand that you should; it is not good manners to push in first, and people people have good manners.

Question 13 – Are you often late?
You know that you should not be; if you are late it shows lack of consideration for other people and their time.

Question 14 – Do you look at people when they are talking to you?
If you are a good people person you are a good communicator, and good communicators have the courage and honesty to look the other person in the eye.

This is a book about being a people person; as you work through the book you will find all these questions are dealt with. If you now know, through doing this quiz, where your weaknesses lie, you will be able to improve on what you are not so good at and pat yourself on the back for the things which you do well.

What makes a person?

We have been talking about whether or not you are a people person, but what goes to make up a person? What do you need to know about a person before you can build up a satisfactory business relationship with him or her?

☐ *Exercise 1*

You can do this for yourself or with a group. Draw a pie chart with 14 equal segments; in each segment write an aspect of a person's life and background which goes to make up that whole being we call a person – the influences which have made that person what they are. Upbringing is one, education is another. Can you fill in the other segments?

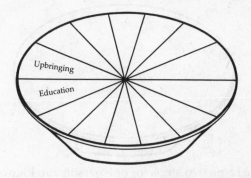

You might have filled in all the segments, or only some of them, or have more than enough to fill the chart, but you can easily see that a person is made up of many parts, all of which have had or are having a greater or lesser influence on them. In the pie chart you have just drawn all the segments are equal, but it is very unlikely that this is true in real life. For some people education is a much greater influence than upbringing, for example, and vice versa for others. For some religion is a very strong influence, for others almost none at all.

The other influences you could have filled in are: religion, present home circumstances, health, money, interests, appearance, work, training, gender (men and women sometimes have a different outlook on life), ability, race, geography, and possibly others.

Now that you have thought about, and written down, the sorts of things which make people what they are, do a comparison between two specific people – yourself and one other person. Do yourself first:

Your name:

Step 1 Think about yourself, and make a list of all the things which have influenced you to make you what you are now. Upbringing and education are bound to be in there somewhere.

<u>LIST</u>

....
....
....
....
....

Step 2 Convert this into a pie chart, but this time do not make the segments equal; give more space to the things which have influenced you more. For example, if you think that religion has had very little influence on you, give it a very small segment.

Now do the same two steps for one person you know reasonably well. They need not be very close to you, and it makes it more interesting if they are fairly different from you. It could be someone in the family, or a friend, or a colleague at school, college or work.

<u>LIST</u>

....
....
....
....
....
....
....
....
....
....

Finally compare the two pie charts, and see how different they look. It will make the differences more apparent if you colour the charts. One will not be better or worse than the other, one will not be right and the other wrong, they will just be different.

Doing this exercise helps people to realise why people are different and why building up good business relationships takes time, thought and effort. People are different and need to be treated differently, but they all need to be treated as people and not just as inhuman cogs in a machine.

The people you deal with

You deal with all sorts of people in your working life: people outside the company or organisation, and people inside the company. The people outside the organisation are usually customers or clients of some sort. They may have different titles like patient, traveller, consumer, pupil, audience, congregation etc, but they are all people to whom you give a service and are clients or customers.

Exercise 2

1 If you have never done so before, make a list of all the people *outside* your organisation with whom you come into contact. They might be the general public, sales reps, personnel from other organisations and so on. If you are at school or college, think of any Saturday jobs or work experience placements you have had.
2 Now make a list of the people you regularly come into contact with *inside* your organisation. They might be other departments, your boss, your colleagues, lecturers, teachers, caterers etc.

Contacts Quiz

Inside my organisation	Outside my organisation

> By the time you have written down all the people, both outside and inside your organisation with whom you are in regular contact, you should have quite a long list.

Ask yourself this question:

DO I TREAT THE PEOPLE *INSIDE* THE ORGANISATION AS WELL AS I TREAT THE PEOPLE OUTSIDE THE ORGANISATION?

In other words, do you look upon your colleagues as customers too? They are, or should be. Look around you now, and ask yourself whether you are as helpful and polite to the people you can see as you are to any external customers or clients with whom you come into contact. Very few people genuinely treat their colleagues as customers, but if everyone did, it would make the business relationships much more satisfactory.

You do not have to go overboard with your friends and colleagues at school, college or work and start addressing them as Mr, Miss etc; internal working relationships are usually good if they are fairly informal. However, you should be looking upon them as people with a need for your help, advice, courtesy and all the other things you would naturally give to people outside the organisation.

COLLEAGUES ARE CUSTOMERS TOO

If you start to treat people in this way, the likelihood is that they will do the same for you. Behaviour breeds behaviour.

What people need from you

If you are to be a good people person, people need several things from you. They need:

(a) Adult behaviour
What does 'adult' behaviour mean? It means acting in a sensible, calm, logical way, sorting things out between you with understanding on **both** sides. If you are yourself managing or supervising others, your staff are your customers, and they need you to treat them in an adult sort of way.

People who have tantrums and start to lose their temper, or are more subtle and are sarcastic or sulky, are acting like spoiled children.

(b) Parenting
Sometimes people need your sympathy and look to you to nurture them
and help them out of a crisis in a motherly or fatherly sort of way, even if
you are quite young. Something as simple as getting them a tea or a
coffee when they are under stress can be what is needed.

Sometimes people need you to tell them what to do, just as a parent
tells a child what to do and how to do it.

(c) Childlike curiosity
The word here is 'childlike' not 'childish'; children are naturally curious,
and if you can channel this natural curiosity into your working life, it
will help you find out about things and be interested in what you and
other people have to do.

Children are also very fun-loving, and it does no harm to bring a bit
of fun into working life occasionally, provided you know how far to go
and when to stop.

(d) Reliability
People need to know they can depend on you for all sorts of things:
● to be on time
● to do what you say you will do
● to meet deadlines
● to be accurate
● not to make promises you cannot keep
● to pass on messages

If you are consistently unreliable it will damage your working
relationships: people will get fed up with you, and will not regard you as
a good person with whom to work.

(e) Good manners
Manners change, and what was considered good manners twenty or
thirty years ago will not necessarily be seen as good manners now. It is
no longer expected that a man should offer his seat to a woman on a
train, for example.

There are many small courtesies, however, which make life run
more smoothly for everyone. It does not matter whether people are
young, old, male, female, experienced, new, holding a very senior
position or carrying out a menial task; if people treat people with
courtesy and good manners, working life is more pleasant for everyone.

Here is a list of things you should always do for everyone, no matter
who they are:
1 Greet them – say hello, good morning etc
2 Smile at them
3 Say please and thank you ('Cheers!' will do)

4 Open doors
5 Hold a door open when you have gone through it – look behind you
to check
6 Let other people go first
7 If other people let you go first, accept with a smile and a thank you
8 Help people lift heavy things
9 Help people get things from high shelves
10 Hand things to them the right way round – towards them rather than
towards you
11 Offer to help people in a difficulty – don't wait to be asked
12 Pick things up for people when they drop them
13 Call people by their name
14 Get people's names right

Practice

If you are going to gain anything from using this book, you need to
improve your areas of weakness and put into practice some of the
things you have been thinking about.

Look back over this chapter now, and decide on **not more than
two things** that you can do to improve your people skills. It might be
as simple as finding out someone's name and using it.

When you have decided on the two things, commit yourself to
doing them by writing them down, in this way, for example:
I will:

1 Remember that . . . . does not have much money, and stop
trying to tempt him/her to spend more
2 Check behind me *every* time I go through a door to see if someone is
following, and if they are, I will hold the door open for them.

Does this sort of thing seem silly to you? It might. But remember
that behaviour breeds behaviour, and you will find that if you become
a real people person, other people will respond by treating you as a
person. It will not happen overnight, but keep working at it, and it
will.

Points to remember from this chapter

- Listen, rather than talking
- Ask for help if you need it
- Don't lose your temper or sound cross
- Be reliable
- People are complex and need understanding
- Everyone is a person
- Courtesy costs nothing
- Colleagues are customers too

2 Gathering Information

In this chapter:
- Listening
- Questioning
- Responding
- Understanding
- Note-taking

This chapter goes in depth into each of the skills listed above, and concentrates on how you can build business relationships, particularly within a company or organisation, by putting these skills into practice.

Listening

When we are children we are taught to speak, read and write, but we are never taught to listen. What most of us get is our parents saying something like 'Look at me when I'm talking to you'. That is a very good and basic lesson to learn, but we are taught little else about listening.

Listening well is a very definite skill which can be learnt and practised. You often hear people say 'Oh, he's great to work with' or 'She's really good to talk to'. When you analyse why people are great to work with or good to talk to, you often find that they are very good listeners, as well as being reliable, interesting and all the other things that make people good to be with.

One of the most important things about listening, when you are in conversation with somebody face-to-face, is to get the body language signals right, and to **show** that you are listening.

Exercise 1

Here is a listening exercise which you can do in pairs of one talker and one listener; it is better if several of you do it simultaneously, because if you are doing this with just one other person, the talker can get embarrassed by the sound of his/her own voice. Set up the exercise like this:

Part A

1 Each pair should sit with their chairs facing each other, but not touching.

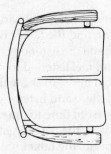 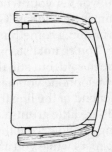

2 One chooses to be the talker and the other the listener.
3 The talker will talk for two minutes on 'A time when I asked for help'. It could be anything from losing your way to breaking down in a car or being unable to do your work.
4 The listener will sit quite still and do nothing **except** look the talker in the eye. Don't fidget or smile or nod. Just sit there looking at the talker. If you think you are going to giggle, grit your teeth. It's very hard to giggle when your teeth are clenched.
5 You should be working in a group of several pairs, and the talkers should all start talking at the same time.
6 At the end of two minutes, let the talker say how s/he felt under this unflinching gaze.

Part B

1 Swap roles now, so that the talker becomes the listener and the listener becomes the talker.
2 This time the talker will talk for two minutes about a problem s/he has. Again, it can be about absolutely anything at home, at work, your hobbies or interests. Personal problems are probably better not spoken about in this situation, although some talkers feel they want to air their personal problems, and they are often the most interesting to listen to!

> 3 The listener may do anything **except** look the talker in the eye this time. You can nod, smile, look up at the ceiling, fidget – anything but look the talker in the eye.
> 4 At the end of two minutes, ask how the talker felt.

Of course these circumstances are exaggerated, but they do show the importance of showing people that you are listening to them, by leaning forward slightly, by nodding and smiling and looking at them. Do not stare at them, or look at them fixedly for too long, or they will feel threatened, but do not let your eyes wander round the room or towards someone else while someone is talking to you. Concentrate on the talker and give him or her your whole attention.

Sometimes people say 'Go on, I'm listening' while they are hunting for papers or doing something quite different, and the talker will feel like saying 'You're **not** listening to me'. Perhaps the listener can repeat what has been said, but still the talker will not feel listened to.

On the telephone you have to give 'verbal nods' to show the person on the other end of the line that you are still there and listening. These verbal nods are little grunts and saying 'Yes' from time to time without interrupting the flow from the other end. If you, the listener, start shuffling papers while you are on the telephone, the talker will soon detect that you are not giving your full attention to the conversation, so if you have to look for something, ask the other person to hang on while you do so and then come back and concentrate on the call.

Rule 1 about listening: Concentrate, and show the talker that you are listening.

Rule 2 about listening: Don't interrupt.

Interrupting is quite different from the verbal nods to show that you are still there. You will want to put your point of view, to question and respond, but if you interrupt the talker in mid-sentence two things are bound to happen:

(a) you will have stopped listening
(b) they will lose their momentum and possibly their train of thought.

It is also rude to interrupt.

Everyone has to pause for breath at some point, and that is when you leap in with your question or response. Unless you are concentrating you will miss the opportunity.

Sometimes you are in a genuine hurry and need to interrupt. At those times, which can sometimes happen in working life, apologise for

interrupting and say what you have to say. You should do this if you
have to butt in on a conversation between other people. Next time your
friends or colleagues are having a serious conversation or just a chat,
notice how often people interrupt each other. It is surprisingly frequent.

Rule 3 about listening: Don't assume.

How often have you heard people say 'Oh, I'm sorry, I assumed
that . . .'?

Exercise 2

Read this conversation and then write down what assumptions the
listener made.

'Come in.'
'Oh, Mr Goodman, I wonder if you could help me . . .'
'Well, I'll try. What's your name, by the way?'
'It's Sarah. Sarah Stewart.'
'Well, Sarah, what can I do for you? You're new here aren't you –
  haven't seen you around before.'
'Well, no, I joined the company six months ago.'
'Oh did you? Well, How can I help? I bet it's about money – it
  usually is with young people starting work.'
'It is in a way . . .'
'Thought so. Tax still in a muddle is it?'
'Yes, it is, but that's not . . .'
'Yes, it usually is. Takes nearly a year to sort out sometimes. Now,
  if I were you I'd go and see Mary Blackmore in wages. She's
  very good at sorting out that sort of thing. You go and see her –
  tell her I sent you.'
'I've already seen Mary, and she's been very helpful, thank you.'
'Oh! Thought you said you had a money problem. If it isn't the
  tax, what is it?'
'I wondered whether you could sign my Petty Cash voucher,
  please. You see, Mr Hart's not in and . . .'

There were at least four assumptions that Mr Goodman made.
What were they?
If you assume, you run the risk of talking about something quite
different from what was intended by the talker, so you waste time
and irritate people.

Mr Goodman's four assumptions were:

(a) That Sarah was new, just because he hadn't seen her
(b) That the problem was about money
(c) That the money problem was about tax
(d) That Sarah had not already seen Mary Blackmore.

If you assume you make an ass of you and me

ASS/U/ME

Rule 4 about listening: Don't let your pre-conceived ideas prejudice you.

In the conversation you have just read Mr Goodman had the pre-conceived idea that young people starting work have money problems, which led him to make his inaccurate assumptions. People find it very difficult not to let their pre-conceived ideas influence their thinking; consequently they do not listen well.

Here are some fairly common pre-conceived ideas, some of which are downright prejudices, sometimes in favour, but more often against:

- older people don't like change
- young people have no consideration
- people of Asian origin are hard workers
- women don't make good managers
- men always know what they want
- doing accounts is boring
- the acting profession is glamorous

What are your prejudices or pre-conceived ideas? Perhaps you find something easy to do, so you assume everyone else will as well. Perhaps there is someone at work you do not like – you still need to listen to them. Perhaps you have heard that a certain person or department is difficult to deal with, so you start off on the defensive and do not listen properly to what they have to say.

Approach each new situation with an open mind; you will listen and get things sorted out much better if you do.

The four basic listening rules are:

1 Concentrate and show that you are listening
2 Don't interrupt
3 Don't assume (ass/u/me)
4 Don't let your pre-conceived ideas influence you.

Questioning

Good and intelligent listening will mean that you want to ask questions to clarify what people have said or to help them reach a decision. The questions are divided into four types so that you can learn how to ask the right questions at the right time and gather the information you need.

The four types of question are:

OPEN — Requires more than a 'yes' or 'no' answer, eg What did that involve? This question makes the talker expand on a previous thought.

CLOSED — Can be answered with a 'yes' or 'no' straight fact, eg Did you have a good journey? This question can be answered 'yes' or 'no' without anything at all being added.

LEADING — Suggests the answer in the question, eg You agree we must do something about it, don't you? This question forces the other person to respond in the way you want them to.

LIMITING — Includes alternative answers in the question, eg Do you prefer tea or coffee? This question helps the other person to make a choice; the choice is limited.

Exercise 3: Questions quiz

Suppose you and your colleague wanted to go out for lunch and you were trying to decide on somewhere which would suit you both. Here is a series of questions you could ask. For each question, tick which type of question it is – OPEN, CLOSED, LEADING OR LIMITING.

	Open	Closed	Leading	Limiting
1 We don't want a lot to eat, do we?				
2 Where would you like to go?				
3 Can you eat fish?				
4 Do you like fish?				
5 Would you prefer hamburgers or fish and chips?				
6 Shall we try the new wine bar?				
7 You'd like to try the new sandwich place, wouldn't you?				
8 How much time have you got?				

Some of these questions leave the field wide open for the other person to state preferences; some limit the choice and two definitely lead the other person in a certain direction. Which was which?

Don't turn over the page until you've decided.

1 is leading, daring the other person to say 'No'
2 is totally open
3 is closed – it can be answered 'yes' or 'no'
4 is also closed. Both these questions are usful in this context: fish has
been eliminated from the menu, or not
5 gives a limited choice
6 is a closed question
7 is definitely leading and
8 is open.

Open questions start with who, what, when, where, why and how.
They encourage the other person to keep talking. If you want more
information, use open questions, but if you want other people to make a
choice, ask closed or limiting questions. Leading questions are often
more of a statement forcing the other person to agree with you, and
should not be used if you genuinely want to gather information.

	Exercise 4

Suppose now that you have been asked to do some work for
tomorrow. You need to know exactly when this work needs to be
completed. Which question would you ask:

OPEN   When do you want it by?
CLOSED   Do you want it finished today?
LEADING   You won't want it until tomorrow afternoon, will you?
LIMITING   Do you want it by 5.30 tonight or will 11.00 tomorrow
            do?

It depends on what your own priorities are which type of question
you would use.

If you genuinely want to know what the deadline is, and can cope with
the work easily, ask the open question – 'When do you want it by?
If you think the work is wanted urgently and you know you can
complete it by the end of the day, ask the closed question – 'Do you
want it finished today?' If the answer is 'yes' and you cannot complete it
yourself, you would be able to say so.
If you are really pushed for time and think that the work is not very
urgent anyway, you could ask the leading question – 'You won't want it
until tomorrow afternoon, will you?'
If you want to pin down exactly at what time the work is needed *and*
show that you are busy anyway, you could ask the limiting question –
'Do you want it done by 5.30 tonight or will 11.00 tomorrow do?'

All this is just to clarify when some work should be completed! But the response will depend on the type of question you ask, and the business relationship between you and the other person will have developed a little further.

Responding

As well as listening and questioning you need to respond. When you respond to a request, a question or just another person's thoughts, your tone of voice is important. You know that you should not sound reluctant, bored, unhelpful and all the rest of it. You know that you should sound helpful, sympathetic, interested, concerned and so on, according to the circumstances. It is not always easy to be and sound positive in all situations, but at least you know what you are trying to be and sound like.

Your tone of voice and general attitude *are* important, but when you are responding, the words themselves are just as important as your tone of voice. The words you use can make you sound sympathetic, interested and someone people like to talk to, or they can make you sound judgemental, impatient, arrogant, patronising and all the other things that can destroy a business relationship.

Exercise 5

If someone says to you 'I really don't know what I'm doing', how would you respond? Here are some responses; because they are written, you have only the words to go on – the body language, the tone of voice do not come into it. For each response write down or say what underlying meaning you think the words convey:

Statement
'I really don't know what I'm doing.'

Responses
1 'Why not, for goodness sake?'
2 'Don't you? Well, I showed you yesterday.'
3 'Yes, that's not so easy, that bit.'
4 'Most people can manage it.'
5 'Yes, I found that difficult.'
6 'Never mind, Jim will do it for you.'
7 'You're normally so good at these things.'

8 'Can I help?'
9 'Yes, I find that difficult. Can I help?'
10 'Yes, I've seen you struggling. Why didn't you ask me to give you a hand?'

What did you think was the underlying message behind those ten responses?

Here is an interpretation with which you may, or may not, agree.

Statement
'I really don't know what I'm doing.'
Response 1 – 'Why not, for goodness sake?'
'You ought to be able to do it, everybody else can. You're stupid.' **A put down.'**
Response 2 – 'Don't you? Well, I showed you yesterday.'
'I obviously wasted my time yesterday. You're stupid.' **Another put down.**
Response 3 – 'Yes, that's not so easy, that bit.'
'I understand why you can't do it. Other people find it difficult too.' **Sympathetic, but that is as far as it goes.**
Response 4 – 'Most people can manage it.'
'You must be stupider than most.' **A put down.**
Response 5 – 'Yes, I found that difficult.'
'I understand, because I've been in the same boat.' **Even more sympathetic, but it still goes no further.**
Response 6 – 'Never mind, Jim will do it for you.'
'I'm sorry you're so incompetent – give it to someone else.' **Hardly encouraging.**
Response 7 – 'You're so good at these things normally.'
'You must be a bit less competent than I thought. Pity.' **A bit patronising and disillusioned.**
Response 8 – 'Can I help?'
'I'm happy to help you.' **This is a bit abrupt, and might imply 'I think you can't cope'.**
Response 9 – 'Yes, I find that difficult. Can I help?'
'I understand, because I've been in the same boat. I needed help then, so I'm happy to help you now.' **Much the best response. Not only sympathetic, but offering to help as well.**
Response 10 – 'Yes, I've seen you struggling. Why didn't you ask me to give you a hand?'
'Poor fool! I've enjoyed watching you wriggling like a worm on a hook, and you hadn't even the courage to ask for help.' **If you really wanted to help, response 9 would have been better; sympathy plus action.**

Next time you feel uncomfortable or put down by someone else, try to analyse what it was that made you feel like that. Tone of voice and body language might have had quite a lot to do with it, but it might, too, have been the words and the underlying message they conveyed. If that can happen to you, do you do the same sort of thing to other people?

If you make the best response to people, you are much more likely to build a satisfactory business relationship. This in turn will make it easier for you to gather information from that person next time you come into contact.

Understanding

People understand things differently, because of the people they are, their background, education and so on. When you are listening to other people, pick up the words which are vague, or which you are not sure you understand, and make sure you clarify them.

Exercise 6

Go round your group and ask them what the following words mean to them:
- soon
- a few
- occasionally
- teenage
- middle aged
- next Friday
- afternoon
- spring/autumn

You will probably have found that all these words mean slightly different things to different people. Communication in business is about being precise, so you must make sure that you check your understanding when other people use vague words like this, and that you do not use imprecise words yourself.

It is important to check deadlines, too. If someone asks you for something 'next Wednesday', do they mean Wednesday of next week or in two days' time? And do they really mean Wednesday, or should whatever it is be finished and delivered by close of business on Tuesday? Take time to check these things, it saves time in the end.

Check people's body language, too. Don't forget that if body language and words do not match, believe the body language, which often tells the true story.

| | *Exercise 7* |

What do these signals convey to you?

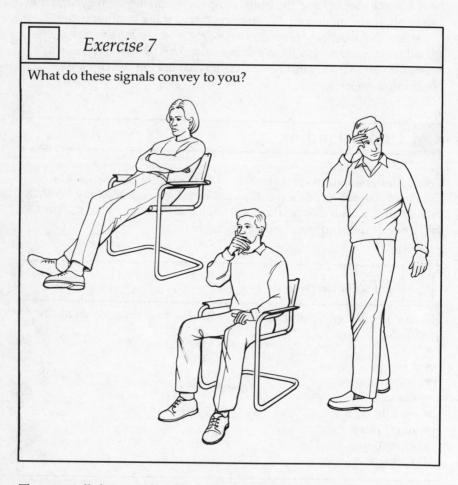

These are all clusters of body language signals which tell you that the person is unsure in some way.

The person sitting with arms folded, pursed lips and legs crossed is looking very closed and unreceptive. If you want to gather information from this person you must do or say something to make them more cooperative.

The person with his hand in front if his mouth might be conveying that he is not too sure of what he is saying. You would need to ask more questions to get at the real truth.

The person looking back, puzzled, is telling you that he has not understood what you have said. Unless you watch people you will not pick up these signals, and will not understand why they were unable to do what you asked.

When you are interpreting the messages that others are conveying to you, you depend a lot on the tone of voice they use. When you are face-to-face the tone of voice combined with the words and body language will tell you the whole story, if you can read it. On the telephone you are restricted to the words and the tone of voice. This means that you have to concentrate and listen even harder to pick up the small hesitations, the negative signs and the lack of understanding that someone is conveying to you.

 # Note-taking

Are you one of those people who write long, rambling notes to yourself during a telephone call and then cannot decipher them afterwards? Are you one of those people who write long, rambling messages to other people so that the facts are hidden somewhere in the depths of the text? Many people are.

If you are to gather information accurately you will need to practise taking notes in a clear, concise way. People do this in individual ways, and it is difficult to guide people on how to take good notes. However, here are some guidelines:

Note-taking guidelines
1 Write down **clearly** name of other person, company, telephone extension etc. Get at least this right and you can always re-establish contact to check what was said.
2 Write headings and underline them so that you know what the main thoughts are. You do not need to write sentences, just words to help you remember what was said. Underneath each heading you can write the important details. For example, if you were trying to arrange a meeting over the telephone with Karen Smith, your notes during the telephone conversation could look something like this:

> Karen Smith x232
> *Meeting*   about new catalogue
> *Venue*   her office
> *Time*   10.00 am
> *Action*   She will tell Pam, Kevin and Peter
> I will tell Dawn and Michael

Once you have put the 'phone down you can make the entries in the

diary, contact Dawn and Michael and so on.
3 Check back: all names
                figures
                action

'What did you say your extension number was? 233? No, 232? OK; and you are going to contact Pam, Kevin and Peter and I'll contact Dawn and Michael. OK. See you in your office at 10.00 on the 22nd then.'

It takes very little time to do this, and can save a lot of time and embarrassment if you get it wrong because you have not checked.
4 Write up the notes or take the action as soon as possible. Your first notes are only rough, so you need to write them in your list of things to do or your diary or wherever else you keep them as soon as you have put the 'phone down. Leave it half a day and you will not be able to read and remember whether you said 10.00 or 10.30 if the figures are not clear.

You can follow these guidelines when you are writing messages for other people. They want facts, not essays, so write what you have to say as briefly as possible, making sure you get all the facts down.

Exercise 8

Read this message, which is too long, and re-write it giving only the facts that the recipient needs. You work in the Department of Education and Science (DES) and are Mr Duncan Frost's secretary; this is the message you have written:

'Miss Hazel Sandys, an Assistant Secretary from the DSS, wants to come and see you about the new schools voucher scheme – she thinks it may well have an adverse effect on the health of the poorer families and create additional strain on the hospital and medical services. Can she come and see you early next week on Monday or Tuesday (Wednesday at the latest)? She wants me to ring her back on 081 407 6678 and she is not sure where the office is. Can you let me know when you want to see her, please – I see you've got a meeting pencilled in for all day Tuesday. Will Monday afternoon be OK? I know you are usually out on Monday afternoons but there's nothing in your diary. I've left Monday morning free as usual.'

It would take Mr Frost a long time to read through all that, so write a clearer, more concise message. Do this without looking at the example opposite, and then compare the two.

'I've booked Miss Hazel Sandys, Assistant Secretary from the DSS, to see you at 2.00 pm on Monday (date). She wants to discuss the effect of the school voucher scheme on poorer families and health services. Please let me know if this is OK so I can ring her back.'

Here you have got all the important facts – date, time, who and why, and have asked Mr Frost to take specific action. There is nothing else he needs to know at this stage.

This chapter about gathering information has been quite long and detailed, but gathering information well is such a fundamental skill in building business relationships that the chapter could not afford to be sketchy. There have been several exercises so there is no formal practice, but you should practise all these skills as they are needed throughout your working life.

Points to remember from this chapter

- Listen with concentration
- Don't interrupt
- If you assume, you make an ass of you and me. ASS/U/ME
- Know your prejudices
- Don't be influenced by pre-conceived ideas
- Use the right type of question – OPEN, CLOSED, LEADING, LIMITING
- Respond with encouragement, not a put down
- Check your understanding of vague words
- Read the body language signals
- Listen to the tone of voice
- When note-taking, write headings and re-check the detail

Further reading

Dealing with customers and clients
Vera Hughes and David Weller, *Self Presentation Skills* (Macmillan, 1991), Chapter 6.
Body language
Alan Pease, *Body Language* (Sheldon Press).
Vera Hughes and David Weller, *Self Presentation Skills* (Macmillan, 1991), Chapter 1.

3 Opening and Closing

In this chapter:
- Territory
- Personal space
- Greeting
  - face-to-face
  - on the telephone
- Parting
  - face-to-face
  - on the telephone
- Positive body language

 ## Territory

Think of the wildlife programmes on the television, and you will realise how much of their lives the animals and birds spend marking out and defending their territory. Human beings are no different. We have our own territory within which we feel safe and secure. We have our homes where strangers do not enter uninvited. You will often hear people who have been burgled say that it is not so much the loss of their property that upsets them as the fact that a stranger has been in their home rooting around among their possessions.

When we are away from home we create little territories for ourselves. Watch people on a beach, spread out with all their possessions around them. When another family or couple stakes out their territory too close, the first-comers will not only glare at the newcomers, but often adjust their possessions to bring them a little nearer. They are defending their territory and warning others to keep off. At work, too, we have our own territory – our private space which is ours, and so does everyone else. We have our own desk, or part of a work bench or a computer and somewhere to put our personal belongings.

Can you detect when someone has been sitting at your place? Many people can, and they feel uncomfortable about it unless they have given the other person permission to be there. An office desk or a shop counter, a bench or any area at work does not normally belong to us, but we still feel it is 'ours' and defend it. We move our possessions (biros, rulers, telephone, if we have one at a desk) to mark out the limits of our territory, and we get quite cross if someone else moves them around. 'Who's been at my desk?', you hear people say, and they promptly re-arrange their things to re-establish their territory.

'Who's been sitting at **my** desk?'

If we are so fussy about our territory, other people must feel the same about theirs. This is why it is so important to build good relationships by not encroaching on other people's territory, by not bursting into their room uninvited, by not borrowing things without asking and so on. If you show respect for their territory, they are more likely to show respect for yours. Behaviour breeds behaviour.

Why do you always sit at the same place at a meeting or in a classroom or lecture room? Because you have made that place your territory, and you feel secure there. If someone pinches your established place, you often feel quite angry about it. So respect other people's feelings in the same circumstances, and if you are new to a meeting or a group, wait to see where others are sitting and do not sit in their favourite spot.

Exercise 1

Discuss with your group, or think for yourself, what irritates or annoys you about other people invading your territory, at home and at work, school or college. It could be someone coming into your bedroom without knocking, or borrowing your tools without asking. Make a list of all these things, and then ask yourself, seriously, how often you irritate other people by doing the same sort of thing yourself.

People sometimes see territory as a sort of power game. For example, they make sure a meeting is in their office (on their territory) where they feel secure and can dominate others if necessary. Perhaps they build barriers between themselves and other people – they use their desk as a natural barrier and they stay behind it. Some people, who must feel very insecure, build barriers and obstacles of files and papers on and around their desks, so that nobody can get near them.

When people come to see you they are entering your territory. When you go to see them, you are entering theirs. This is why it is so important to make visitors welcome, to come out from behind the barrier and to invite them into your territory. If you are going into a room where someone is normally welcoming and friendly, but this time you find them behind the desk, looking stern, watch out – you are probably in for a rough time.

Of course it is not possible to come round from behind the desk every time someone walks into your room, but if it is a stranger, or someone very senior to you, you should try to do this to make them welcome.

 ## Personal space

In addition to our territory, which we take care to establish and defend, we all have around us a little area of personal space, and we feel even more threatened if someone enters that space uninvited.

Some people feel uncomfortable if other people touch them, and meeting a stranger's eyes can be embarrassing. These are two ways of invading someone's personal space – by touch and by eye contact. This is why we try to avoid touching each other in a crowd or as we pass on the pavement. At work it is important to recognise other people's personal space, and not to enter that space uninvited. Here are a few DOs and DON'Ts which will make you and other people feel more comfortable:

DO
- Approach someone from the front, if possible, not from the side or behind. Take the trouble to walk round to the front so that they can see you coming.
- Let someone take something from you rather than thrusting it at them. If you offer it and they accept it, they will draw it in to their own personal space.
- Shake hands, if appropriate. It is a good way of breaking down barriers and entering someone's personal space without giving offence.

DON'T
- Stand too close to people.
- Hover behind someone just out of their view.
- Touch people if either of you feels uncomfortable about it.
- Stare at people while they are working.
- Jostle people as you move about. Stand aside and let them pass, if necessary.
- Lean over someone's shoulder, if you can help it.

No-one likes anyone who is inconsiderate or forceful in a physical way. Have respect for other people's personal space.

The amount of personal space a person needs varies from culture to culture and from town to country. People who live in towns, for example, or people who live a crowded sort of life, like the Japanese, are used to squashing up, and their personal space is quite small. People from the country, or Australians, for example, where there are wide open spaces and people are not living on top of one another, need much more personal space to feel comfortable. If you bear this in mind when you are dealing with people from different parts of the country or the world, you can adapt your behaviour to their needs.

What can you do if someone with whom you work is continually invading your territory or your personal space and really irritating you? If this happens, do something about it, however difficult the situation is. Perhaps they are annoying you unnecessarily or perhaps they are deliberately harassing you. In either case it is foolish to let it go on, because it will make you very unhappy and certainly less productive at work. So what can you do? The first thing you have to do is tell them. What should you say? The words to use will vary from person to person, but you should always choose a moment when you are feeling calm and rational and can say what you have to in a matter-of-fact and unemotional tone of voice. Try saying something like: 'Look, I don't know if you realise this, but I get a bit uptight every time you borrow my pen without asking. Do you think you could ask next time, please?' If the other person has not realised s/he is doing this s/he will probably say sorry and thanks for saying so.

The words you use are important, as well as the tone of your voice. If you can convey that you are upset by something someone else does, rather than accusing them of upsetting you, they will find it easier to accept. You are indicating that it is you who have the problem, not they, so the emotional temperature is less likely to rise.

If the irritation becomes really serious and turns into sexual harassment – and this can happen to young people starting out in working life – you cannot let it go on. You can change jobs, but that will not solve the situation for anyone else, and maybe you like your job anyway. You have to be firm and tell the person harassing you that you cannot work in such circumstances. Say something like 'Look, I don't like you touching me up, please don't do it'. Speak calmly and quietly, but be positive and firm about it. If the harassment continues, turn to someone else in the company for help – there is usually someone you can tell. Be calm and factual if you can, although it will probably be a very difficult thing to do. If there is no-one to turn to and you cannot see your way out of the situation, look for the Help Lines in your local *Thomson's*. Do something, not nothing.

Greeting

Chapter 2 of *Self Presentation Skills* goes into quite a lot of detail about how to approach people in various situations, and what you should do when other people approach you. Here we shall be thinking particularly about the words you use to external and internal customers (colleagues); you know that the tone of your voice should be friendly and that your body language should be open and welcoming.

Face-to-face

Exercise 2: First words quiz

Think about the words you use and write down the first words you would say to the following people who are coming to see you – entering your territory. It is a normal working day.

What you would say first

1 The head of your establishment (manager, head master, head mistress, principal etc)

2 Someone visiting from another organisation

3 Your colleague you work with every day

4 Your immediate boss/lecturer/teacher

5 Somebody junior to you

6 The cleaner or caretaker

7 A customer in your shop

8 Someone you work with, but don't like

9 A stranger looking lost

> When you have written this down, discuss what you wrote with the others in your group, or analyse it on your own.

It is unlikely that you would say the same to each of those people, but for each you should start with good morning, good afternoon, hello or hi! – whichever is appropriate. If you plunge straight into conversation people are taken a little by surprise – they need a moment to tune into your thoughts. Use people's names whenever you can because it sounds friendly and encouraging and acknowledges them as a person.

Was there anyone on the list you would not normally greet at all? There is no reason to miss anyone out. You might try greeting the person selling you your train ticket or the checkout operator too, if you do not already do this. Try it; it makes life more pleasant for them and for you.

If you see a stranger wandering about it is sometimes important from a security point of view to 'challenge' them by greeting them and asking if there is anything you can do to help. If they are genuinely lost they will appreciate your help. If they are up to no good it will show them that you are alert, and they will normally move on swiftly.

On the telephone

What do you say when you answer the telephone? There is usually a convention or way of doing it in your particular establishment; if there is, follow it. If there is not, you should do this:
- Give a greeting – good morning, or good afternoon
- Give your name or job title
- Give your company/department etc

Say a greeting **first**, before you give your name. It gives the caller time to tune in to your voice and ensures that you have got the handset near your mouth before you say the important part – your name and department. Do not say only 'Hello', it is abrupt and can sound rude: you never know who the caller will be. In some organisations the convention is that you follow your greeting and your name with 'How may I help you?'. If that is the convention, follow it.

What do you do when you are answering someone else's 'phone? People often find it difficult to know quite what to say. From the caller's point of view the most helpful thing you can do is this sort of thing: 'Good morning/afternoon, John Smith's 'phone, Phil Butler speaking'. It tells the caller that s/he has got through to the right extension, that that person is not there and the name of the person who is speaking. The caller can then leave a message or ring back without having the embarrassment of asking whether it is the right extension and who you are. Put yourself in the caller's shoes and think what would be most helpful to him or her.

If you yourself are the caller:

- Give a greeting
- Say who you are
- Say where you are from
- Say roughly what you want

Do not plunge straight into detail without checking that you are speaking to the right person. If you follow this sequence it will save you a lot of time, frustration and embarrassment.

Parting

When you have finished your business, you need to part on good terms, each knowing exactly what is going to happen next. You will probably have to work with the other person again, so the way you complete what you have to do and leave the other person is the first step towards the next meeting. If parting is too hasty, frosty or aggressive even, it will make the next meeting more difficult, and at work you cannot necessarily choose the people with whom you are going to be in contact.

Face-to-face

Exercise 3

Here are three 'what would you do next?' scenarios. Read the description of what has happened so far and then write down what **you** would do next. Work with a neighbour or on your own.

1 You have been into your Manager's office to collect some papers. She has told you what she wants, the atmosphere is OK and you are just about to go out of the door. She stops you, because she wants to add something. What would you do next?

2 You are showing a visitor out of the building and have reached the main exit door. You both pause a moment to exchange the final words. What would you do next?

3 You have been attending a small, informal meeting of about six people at which each of you has agreed to take some specific action. You are not totally sure what **you** are supposed to be doing. Everyone stands up to leave. What would you do next?

These are ideas about what you could have done. They are not necessarily right for your circumstances, but they give some guidelines.

1 If you are going out of a door and someone calls you back to add something:
   - stop
   - turn right round
   - listen and acknowledge that you have understood
   - turn round and go out

   You would not be rude enough to keep going without stopping, but you might just stop and turn you head. If you do this your body language is not conveying to the other person that you are fully paying attention. This is because your brain is often focused in the direction in which your feet are pointing. If you turn right round, the person who has stopped you will feel quite confident that you have heard and understood.

2 When you are showing a visitor out say some friendly words like 'Goodbye, nice to have met you'. This is becoming a stock phrase and can be irritating, like 'Have a good day', but you can say it if you really mean it. Shake hands with your visitor if you can. If you are not used to doing this it takes courage and practice, but it does round off a business meeting well and in effect says 'It was nice doing business with you'. Open the door for your visitor, show him or her out and wait, still looking at your visitor until s/he has turned the corner, gone out of sight or is at least a fair way away from you. If you shut the door and go back into your building immediately your visitor will feel cut off.

3 Stand up with the others, showing you are ready to leave, but go up to the leader of the meeting and ask if you can take a minute or two to clarify something. It is much better to get it clear at this stage than to go away and try to work in the dark. It is rare that a meeting leader cannot spare a couple of minutes to sort out a minor problem, but if s/he is really rushed, sort out a time when the two of you can get together. Do stand up as if ready to leave. If you stay sitting down you will look awkward and isolated. When the problem has been sorted, thank the meeting head for the extra time and go promptly to do what you have to. Lingering to chat looks unbusinesslike.

The guidelines from these scenarios can be drawn together for the conclusion of all business transactions:
- Be clear what is to happen next, and check if necessary
- Do not leave until the business has been fully completed

- Say goodbye and thank you
- Shake hands if appropriate
- Don't show visitors out too quickly

On the telephone

The same guidelines apply to the end of a telephone conversation. It is important that you:
- Repeat who is to do what next
- Check names, addresses and figures
- Say thank you and goodbye
- Don't cut the other person off abruptly

If you imagine the person on the other end of the 'phone finishing the call, you will know how they feel when they put the 'phone down. Will they know exactly what to do next? Will they feel friendly towards you, or will they feel hurried and put down? If you start talking to someone else before you put the 'phone down your end, your caller will feel shut out, just as the visitor feels when you shut the door too quickly.

Next time you feel uncomfortable when a 'phone call is finished, try to analyse why. What did you do, and what did the other person do or say? Did the call end in a friendly manner, or did the other person bark down the 'phone at you and almost cut you off in mid-sentence? If you find that sort of thing unpleasant, so will other people.

You have no body language to help you, so on the 'phone you need to concentrate and really get the words, timing and tone of voice right.

Positive body language

If you have read the first chapter of *Self Presentation Skills* you will know how important body language signals are, and that we pick them up subconsciously all the time.

When you are opening or closing a business conversation you need to send out positive body language signals. People usually do this well with external customers, but forget that business transactions with internal customers (colleagues) are just as important.

These drawings show positive body language signals which will make the other person feel at ease.

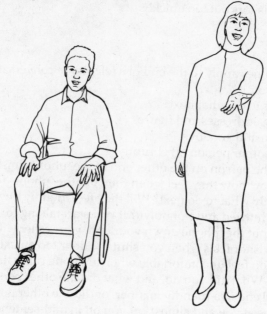

These two people are much more inviting than these two.

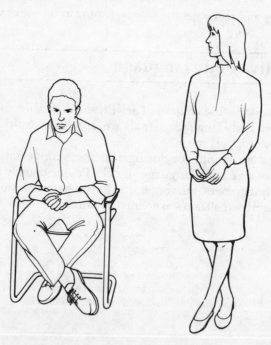

Practice

The next time you go to see someone senior to you, notice what they do and say, and write down the answers to these questions:

1 How were they sitting or standing?

2 Did you feel welcome or a nuisance?

3 How did they greet you?

4 What did they say and what tone of voice did they use?

5 How did they indicate that the meeting was finished?

6 How did you feel as you left?

Remember what you liked and what you did not like about the meeting. Ask yourself whether you do any of the things you did not like. If you can pinpoint what made you feel uncomfortable you will be able to make sure that you do not do the same sort of thing.

Points to remember from this chapter

- We all have our territory and personal space
- Respect other people's territory and space
- Do not put up with irritating behaviour or harassment – do something about it
- Greet people and use their names
- On the telephone, give the greeting before giving your name
- At the end of a meeting check that you know what to do next
- Leave people feeling comfortable and friendly
- Use positive body language signals

38

 Further reading

Approaching people
Vera Hughes and David Weller, *Self Presentation Skills* (Macmillan, 1991),
Chapter 2.
Body language
Vera Hughes and David Weller, *Self Presentation Skills* (Macmillan, 1991),
Chapter 1.

4 Self-preservation Skills

In this chapter:
- The overpowering boss
- The indecisive boss
- Meeting deadlines
- How to say 'no' – and mean it
- Unfulfilled expectations

This chapter is about surviving in a difficult business environment. Most people are helpful and understanding, particularly when you are new to a job, but some people are difficult to work with. The guidelines in this chapter will help you to look at people as people – which is what they are. They are people with difficulties, rather than difficult people.

Sometimes working life can almost seem like a battleground, but you should aim to get to a WIN/WIN situation, rather than a WIN/LOSE situation on either side. You will have to use all your people skills to achieve this, but if you can manage to work with someone whom nobody else can stand, you will certainly be able to look upon yourself as a winner.

You have to know, too, when to say 'enough is enough'; sometimes there are situations when a change of job or a change of boss is the only solution. If you have done all you can to reach a WIN/WIN situation but know that in the end you cannot go on, you will feel justified in making the change.

The overpowering boss

People are overpowering for different reasons and in various ways, but there is no doubt they can be very frightening. You might find yourself afraid of what they will do, but normally you are afraid of what they will say, the unkind or hurtful remarks they will make or the fact that they shout at you. How can you survive in this sort of situation?

First of all, try to sort out in your own mind why your boss is overpowering and a bit frightening. There are four types of overpowering boss. Read about the four types and decide which is yours.

Type A – No time for anyone
This is the type of person who is genuinely very busy, is always in a rush and who gives instructions very quickly, expecting you to understand and act straight away. They do not seem to have time to explain things properly and are surprised when you try to ask them something.

This type of person is often not a good manager of his or her own time. They rush from one crisis to the next, fail to plan what they will do, cannot delegate properly and generally make everyone around them feel exhausted.

What can you do? Several things.

1 Recognise the type of person they are and play the game their way to a certain extent. Do not let them fluster you by rushing around; stay as calm as you can.

2 When they are giving you instructions, concentrate like mad, and if there is something you do not understand, say so then and there. Stop them in their tracks if necessary.

3 If there are several things you need to ask about during a day or a week, have them written down and try to pin your boss down for about a quarter of an hour to answer your queries. You must have them straight in your own mind first, and be able to ask direct questions quickly. Do not worry your boss with things you can find out about somewhere else. You might be able to 'book' a specific time each day or each week.

4 Suggest that your boss uses some other method of letting you know what is wanted than just telling you. Perhaps your boss could jot down a list of things to be done, or could dictate them into a small dictaphone, so that you could listen to them at your own pace.

5 Build up business relationships with someone else in the job so that you can go to them for help about details.

6 As you become more competent in the job, gradually take over some of the small jobs you can do on your own. This will save the boss's time and build up your own reputation.

Type B – The put down
This is the type of boss who is always putting you down or patronising you. They say things like 'Can't you do a simple job like that?!' or 'How many times have I got to tell you . . .' or 'Run along, my dear, and I'll get someone else to see to it'.

Most people get angry occasionally, particularly if you have made a mistake in your work, but this type of boss keeps on putting you down so that you lose your self-confidence and end up believing you are incapable of doing anything.

What can you do?

1 Hang on to your self-confidence, and believe in yourself.

2 Realise that your boss might be feeling insecure in his/her job because of incompetence or lack of knowledge, and is taking it out on you.

3 Your boss might have certain prejudices about your race or your age. This is their problem, not yours. You can feel sorry for their inability to see others as people.

4 Stand up to them and be firm in your own ideas. This does not mean shouting at them, but being able to say something like 'I know you told me how to do this the other day, but I want to get it right; could you explain it again, please' or 'I thought I had done this just the way you wanted it – can you tell me which bit I did wrong, please'. If you are confident that you **can** do something, say so. Say something like 'I'm sure I can do this if you will let me work it out for myself. May I come and show you when I've finished it?'

5 If your boss is sarcastic about you in front of other people this can be a real put down. Your boss might say something like 'Young John here thinks he knows it all – thinks he can run the business single-handed', and leave you feeling about two inches high. What your boss is doing is showing off in front of somebody else.
This is a difficult one to manage, but if you feel able to tell your boss, when you are next alone together (perhaps when you are having an Appraisal discussion – see Chapter 10), how you feel and that you know very well that you have a lot to learn, it might help to improve matters. If matters do not improve, try to ignore the sarcasm and think to yourself that your boss, not you, is the person with the problem. Being sarcastic back hardly ever works.

6 Find something that your boss does well and show that you think it was well done. Say something like 'I learnt a lot from the way you did

that – thanks'. Behaviour breeds behaviour, and next time your boss might remember to praise you instead of putting you down. You must mean what you say, though.

Type C – The shouter

This is the type of person who shouts and probably shouts a lot. They are doing this in order to look big, rather like a frog puffing itself up and croaking loudly. People with real authority rarely have to shout or swear.

If people swear a lot it is often because they have not got a very wide vocabulary, so use swear words because they cannot think of any other words. They do this sometimes to be in fashion, or they do it to look big. It depends what you mean by swear words, of course.

What can you do if this type of behaviour bothers you?

1 Remember the reasons for the shouting and swearing: your boss is probably an inadequate sort of person.

2 Do not shout or swear back. If you both lose control you will never get to a WIN/WIN situation.

3 Set yourself a limit to the amount of shouting or swearing you will take; talk to others about it and see what sort of limit they would set. If the limit is overreached, you can feel free to ask to stop working for your boss, knowing that you have the backing of the others behind you. Nobody has to put up with totally unreasonable behaviour.

4 If the shouting and swearing gets too much during one 'conversation', say something like 'I'm sorry, I do not have to listen to this. I'll come back later' and walk quietly away. Either your boss will seek you out or you will have to go back later and explain precisely why you left – that you feel you cannot concentrate or do your best work if you are shouted at or sworn at. It takes courage to do this, but it often works.

Type D – The brilliant person

Some people are overpowering because they are so brilliant, and they leave you way behind. They simply cannot see how other people cannot understand their thinking. They are not necessarily impatient or arrogant, just better at their work than everyone else around them.

What can you do?

1 Admire them for their brilliance and pity them for their lack of understanding.

2 Learn as much as you can from them.

3 Explain, politely, that you do not understand what they are saying and ask them to go through it again – slowly. Ask questions about things you do not fully understand.

4 When you do understand, thank them for their time and trouble. They will probably feel very pleased with themselves and with you.

Exercise 1

(a) With your neighbour or your colleague at work, think of somebody you know you really would not like to work for.

(b) Try to analyse **why** you would not like to work for them. Do they put people down, shout or swear? Are they too busy to bother with you or too brilliant to notice you? There may be other reasons.

(c) Between you, draw up a plan of how you would tackle the situation, using the guidelines you have just read.
If the situation is for real you must do this anyway, because you cannot do your best work for someone who frightens you.

The indecisive boss

These people can be a real pain to work for. They refuse to take decisions, are incapable of taking decisions, are often late, cannot find things, work in a muddle and keep changing their mind. What you want from your boss is clear direction, and you do not get it.

If you are new to a job you will only gradually realise that your boss is indecisive, because you will not know enough about the work to understand what should be done. Untidy working and lateness sometimes give you a clue, but some very decisive people are untidy or late, so you will have to watch for other signs as well.

What can you do about someone who cannot make up their mind, or who keeps changing it?

1 Decide, when you know enough about the job, which are the really important decisions to be made, and help your boss to make them.

Tell your boss that you need to know the decision so that you can do your work properly. Put the facts before your boss – write them down if necessary – and ask him or her to make the decision.
Keep going until the decision is made.

2 Offer limiting choice – like the limiting questions described in Chapter 2. For example, instead of saying 'What would you like to drink?', say 'Would you like tea or coffee?' You might even ask a leading question like 'I'll make you some coffee, shall I?'
This may sound a very simple situation, but indecisive people often cannot make up their minds about even as small a thing as what they want to drink. They are often trying to do what is best for others, or be very accommodating, instead of saying straight out what they would prefer.
If you carry this through into the important work decisions – ie offer a definite choice between two or, at the most, three different paths to take – the indecisive person will usually choose one or the other, or may come up with something quite different. It might not be what you suggested, but at least a decision will have been made.

3 If you work for someone who keeps changing their mind about where to put things or how to write things, making extra work for you, how can you make them get it right the first or second time, instead of the third or fourth?
At the first change of mind, do not just do as you are told, ask why the change is to be made, so that **you** can get it right next time. If you keep asking questions and so get your boss to think through the problem from every angle, s/he will probably come up with a sensible decision, and you can take the action.

In all these situations, you are helping your boss make up his or her mind. This is rather a frustrating way of working, but it will certainly help you to be decisive, and you can learn a lot from it.

Exercise 2

This is a short case study for you to work through. Do it on your own or with your neighbour.
Ken Baron is an Executive Officer in a local government department. He has received a memo from the Personnel Department reminding him that he must complete the annual holiday form and send it back to Personnel by the end of next week.
   He has had this form for ages, but has not got round to

completing it. You want him to get it done so that you can get your own holiday settled.

Ken has four members of staff:

- **Lucy**, who is 23 and hoping to go on holiday with her boyfriend
- **Clark**, who is 26 and single
- **Tom**, who is 30, married with two small children, and
- **You**, who have been there six months.

The others have given up trying to get Ken to do things on time, but you are determined to get at least this done.

What would you do to get Ken to make the decision, without treading on anyone else's toes and without letting him think that you are too big for your boots? As you decide, think about:

- what Ken needs to know
- what he needs to do
- how you can persuade him to do it
- how you can keep the others on your side.

Write your decisions down.

When you have decided what to do and written it down, compare your thoughts with these. You could:

(a) Ask the others if their holidays are fixed, because you want to fix yours. Agree all the holidays among you.

(b) Agree with them that you will tackle Ken about it.

(c) Go to Ken and say you know he has got the holiday job to do, and can you help.

(d) Would he like you to give him all the information so that he can do the form, or do the form ready for his signature.

If you take these steps you will have consulted with the others and got their go-ahead, collected all the information necessary to do the job, acknowledged to Ken that it is his job, but offered to help, and given him a definite choice of two paths. Finally, you will not have undermined his authority because you will have acknowledged that the form requires his signature.

 ## Meeting deadlines

One of the things that can make life very difficult for you, particularly if your place of work is very busy, is if different people keep giving you work all at once and all of it is 'urgent'.

Try to sort out exactly who you are working for and whose work takes priority. If you are in real difficulties, go to that person, explain the situation and ask for help. If you want to sort the problem out for yourself follow this sequence:

1 Do not do the work in the order in which it is given to you.

2 Ask the person who is giving you the work when the deadline is. Make sure that the person is very specific and keep asking questions (see Chapter 2) until you get a definite answer.

3 Explain what other work you have to do and the order in which you intend to do it, including the work just given to you.

4 If the work is really urgent, say that you will have to check with the others first, but that you will do your best to get it done quickly. If the work is for your immediate boss, or someone really important, ask him or her to clear it with the others for you.

5 If the deadline is really impossible, say so but suggest an alternative. 'I really shan't be able to get it done by tonight, but I'll do it first thing in the morning and then we can fax it through', is the sort of thing you could say.

6 If, as you work, you can see you are not going to meet an agreed deadline, re-negotiate it. Contact the person for whom you are doing the work, explain the situation and agree a new, more realistic deadline. It is much better to do this than come right up against the deadline and miss it. People are usually reasonable and they will appreciate your concern. Very few deadlines cannot be re-negotiated.

7 Finally, if you are really overwhelmed with work, ask for help. Remember it is a strength, not a weakness, to be able to do this.

 ## How to say 'no' – and mean it

Do you find it easy to say 'no' to people? A lot of people do not. Sometimes you have to say 'no' to someone at work and really mean it. If you are new to the job it is not easy to get the balance right between being willing and helpful and being put upon. Some people who have been in a job a long time and have done more than their fair share of the work, finally decide that enough is enough and that they must put their foot down and say 'no'. For them, too, it is not easy because they are used to being obliging and the people for whom they work are used to them 'helping out' all the time.

Follow this sequence, which in many ways is like the sequence for setting and re-negotiating deadlines.

1 Decide when enough is enough and you can justifiably say 'no'. You do not want to become known as 'The abominable no-man (or woman)', but sometimes people unthinkingly ask you to do something which you are not capable of doing or have not got the time to do. Sometimes you are asked to stay behind yet again and to miss another meeting with your friends.

2 When the time comes to say 'no', say something like 'I'm sorry, I can't do that because . . .' and then give your good reasons. Say it firmly, and mean it.

3 Suggest an alternative. 'I'm sorry, I can't do that because . . . , but I can do . . .'.

4 If you find it really difficult to say the words 'I'm sorry, I can't do that' or whatever the right words are for you, **practise** saying them aloud, over and over again. Do this in your room, or in the bath – somewhere private. It is known as the cracked record method. If you practise saying those words often enough you will find they come out of your mouth automatically when the right time comes to use them.

5 If you are polite but firm people will respect your decision. If you are off-hand or rude and say things like 'No way, you've got to be joking', they will get angry and the business relationship deteriorates. After that it is more difficult to build up again.

Unfulfilled expectations

Some jobs are not all they are cracked up to be. Some job interviews are very unsatisfactory, and tell you little about the job you will actually be doing. Others paint far too rosy a picture and you find that what sounded like the beginning of a good career is really a boring, dead-end job. Occasionally you get stuck with people with whom you really cannot work. You have given it a fair go but are making no progress with them or with your work.

What can you do?

This is where you have to be very honest with yourself and make some hard decisions, but you must make the right decisions or you will jump out of the frying pan into the fire.

48

Do this on your own or with a friend whose judgement you trust. **Write down:**

1 The reasons why you are not happy where you are. Be very honest and ask yourself whether the 'fault' is in any way your own.

2 Whether there is anything more you can do to make your present job acceptable. If the answer is 'yes', write down what you can do and when you intend to do it. If the answer is 'no', go on to the next step.

3 What you are seeking: better prospects, nicer people, more money, a total change of career, or anything else.

4 Whether you can achieve these things with your present employer, but in another part of the business, or whether you need to change jobs.

5 What **you** must do next to achieve your aims. This could be an appointment with your boss or the Personnel Department to explain your problems. Sometimes people in authority know of openings which will be coming up and can consider you for these, particularly if you have expressed an interest in doing something different.
It could be that you do need to change jobs, in which case you must start the job hunt all over again. This time you will have the advantage of knowing how to go about it and at least something about what you do not want to do. Take the decision and go for it.

All this is common sense, but writing it down helps to clarify things for you and helps you to come to a sensible decision. It might be, in the end, that you see your present job as a means to a very good end, and decide to stick to it, but you will have made a definite decision to do this and the job will instantly become more acceptable to you. On the other hand you might decide that you must do something different, and you will have made the beginnings of a plan to help you do it.

You are at work for a large proportion of your life, and you need to do work which you enjoy and which gives you the personal and financial rewards you want, as far as that is possible.

Points to remember from this chapter

- If you are frightened of your boss, analyse what you are frightened of (what type your boss is), decide what to do about it and do it
- Learn all you can from the situations you find yourself in, and promise yourself never to make those mistakes when you become a manager
- Help indecisive people to make decisions by collecting the facts and offering them limited choices
- Make deadlines specific and re-negotiate if necessary
- Decide when enough is enough and practise saying 'I'm sorry, I can't'. Remember the cracked record
- Do not become the 'abominable no-man (or woman)'
- If you really cannot continue with your present job, write down the reasons, the alternatives and your plans
- Go for it

5 People with Difficulties

In this chapter:
Dealing face-to-face and on the 'phone with people who
- are angry
- are aggressive/abusive
- are interrupters
- are compulsive talkers
- do not speak good English
- don't want to know
- have disabilities
- are timid

People are sometimes difficult to deal with, but if you can think of them as people with difficulties, rather than difficult people, you are more likely to be in control of the situation.

In this chapter we shall be looking at ways of dealing with people with difficulties, there will be very general hints and tips, and you must use those which best suit you and your personality and the situation in which you find yourself. The important thing throughout is to try to stay in control of yourself, and so keep your own self-respect.

There will be no exercises as you go through this chapter, but an opportunity for self-analysis and practice at the end of it.

People who are angry

Face-to-face

People who are angry at work are often your internal customers – the people you come into contact with regularly at work. However, if you work in a shop or on public transport, or anywhere where you come into contact with the general public, you will sometimes have to deal with them when they are angry.

In some ways they are easier to deal with if they are your external customers, because their anger is normally not directed at you personally, but at the company or organisation for which you work. In these circumstances you can be quite detached about it, and even sympathetic with them sometimes, so their anger does not leave an unpleasant atmosphere.

With colleagues it is a different matter, depending on the cause of the anger. Sometimes they will be feeling frustrated, or tired or angry about something else, and take it out on you. In that case you can treat them as though they were external customers, knowing that their anger is not directed at you personally.

It is more difficult to deal with if you are the cause of the anger – if you have done something wrong and someone is justifiably angry with you. If you have made a mistake, you need to acknowledge it, say you are sorry and do something about putting it right. In fact this is a good way of dealing with anyone who is angry, in any situation, but first you have to let them run out of steam.

If someone is angry, they have probably got worked up about something and are ready for a shouting match; alternatively they are cold and icy in their anger, but still have things they want to say, perhaps in a jabbing and sarcastic sort of way. If they are standing and you are sitting, stay sitting down for a while – if you stand up immediately, it can look confrontational; this does not apply if you would usually stand up out of respect for their position. In all cases a good way of dealing with the situation is:
- keep calm
- let them talk
- don't interrupt
- wait until they have calmed down enough to listen
- try to sort out the facts
- if there has been a mistake, apologise
- do something to sort the matter out: get the person's mind off what went wrong and onto what you are going to do about it between you

This is easier said than done. Behaviour breeds behaviour, and you will often feel you want to shout or say hurtful things back; you will feel you want to go on the defensive, if you have made a mistake, and find all sorts of reasons why things went wrong. It is a very natural thing to do, but if you do, you have lost control of the situation, and it will take an extra effort to get back on good working terms with the other person.

If you have had a really bad day, it is very difficult not to let things get to you, and you might end up in tears. If you are genuinely upset, it does not matter if you cry, whether you are a man or a woman. Tears might help you get rid of your own anger and frustration, and when you have recovered, you will be able to go back and deal with the situation. What you should not do is use tears as a weapon, particularly if you are a woman dealing with a man. If the man realises you are crying to gain an advantage, he will lose respect for you, and the working relationship will become even more difficult.

On the 'phone

Deal with people on the 'phone who are angry in just the same way: let them talk until they have run out of steam. You do not even need to give the verbal nods mentioned in Chapter 2 if they are really going on; if you just stay quiet, they will eventually stop and say 'Are you still there?' At that point you can begin to have a sensible conversation.

Silence can be useful on the 'phone. It allows time for things to sink in, for people to collect their thoughts and start again. Sometimes they will come back fighting again, but more often than not their anger will have gone down at least a notch or two.

Do not put the 'phone down on people who are angry (which is different from being abusive, which we shall be looking at in the next section). Once you have put the 'phone down, the line of communication is broken **by you**, and you will find it difficult to pick up the 'phone and start again. If someone else puts the 'phone down on you, ring back straight away; **they** have put the 'phone down and will find it difficult to ring back, so you must take the step for the two of you. If you leave it, it will get more and more difficult to re-open the communication link. If you are not communicating you cannot maintain or build the business relationship, unless you can go and talk to them and sort it out face-to-face, which is sometimes possible.

People who are aggressive – face-to-face

People who are actually aggressive – that is threatening you with violence – are fortunately very rare.

If you are likely to be in a situation where you are threatened, you will be told the proper security procedures and there will be good backup support. These sorts of situations could be in a bank, building society or post office when you are behind the counter, in a probation, welfare or unemployment benefit office or where people come feeling aggrieved. For example, a man who did not like the look of his electricity bill arrived at the electricity company's area office with a shotgun. If you are in that sort of situation do what you have been told to do and leave the threatening person to the experts; keep calm and wait for help.

The sort of person you are most likely to meet at work who is in any way physically threatening is a drunk. Drunks can be very frightening, because they are loud and pushy. You are more likely to meet them if you are dealing with the public than if you are working in an office. If you have to deal with a drunk, or a group of drunks, do not try to argue with them. Keep calm and agree with them, and then try to get help. You can leave them while you go to find your manager, unless they are threatening someone else; try to get help as soon as you can. Do not try to deal with them on your own.

Sometimes you can ignore them, and they will go away – it depends on the circumstances. If you work in a shop or some other public place you have to try to protect the other customers from annoyance, so tell the other customers what you are going to do, and get help.

If they are swearing and being really offensive, try not to be provoked. Turn a deaf ear and keep your cool. The words they are using are only words: it is the interpretation we give them that makes them offensive. If they are swearing at you in a foreign language, you would not even know you were being sworn at. The swear words they use are their problem, not yours. Keep calm, and you will stay in control; they are certainly not in control if they are drunk.

 ## People who are abusive – on the 'phone

The same applies to people who swear at you on the 'phone – they are out of control, you are not.

As was suggested in Chapter 4 (the overpowering boss), if you work in a situation where you are likely to receive abusive 'phone calls, agree with your colleagues how many swear words or what sort of abuse is acceptable, and when it goes beyond the limit, you can feel free to put the 'phone down. Put it down gently, do not bang it down, and you will still be in control.

You might be able to say to the caller 'I don't think we can get any further with this matter at the moment; I'll ring you back at . . .', and state a definite time. Then you will have to ring back at the time you said.

If you are threatened on the 'phone with violence, you could say 'Could you just repeat that, please, and I'll just turn the tape on so that our conversation is recorded'. That usually has an immediate effect, because in threatening they are committing a criminal offence anyway.

There is one really important thing to remember when you have been dealing with aggressive or abusive people on the 'phone or face-to-face, and that is the effect on you. Some people, who are used to doing that sort of work, will not be affected by it at all, but most people, particularly if it is not something that happens often, will feel very shaken and will need to take time to recover. We all do this in different ways; for some a few tears in private will help; others need a strong cup of tea, while others need to talk about it at length. Try to know what is best for you, and make sure that you take time out to recover. Explain to other people, if you have to. It is nothing to be ashamed of, and until you have recovered you will not be able to work properly.

Also, if you see that a colleague has been in a stressful situation, respect their need to recover. Offer help, or a sympathetic ear, or a cup of coffee, but if they just want to be left alone, respect that, too.

This sort of thing does not happen very often.

 Interrupters – face-to-face and on the 'phone

Interrupters (people who interrupt) are different from interruptions. Interruptions are things which happen which interrupt the smooth flow of work. If you are a clerk or a secretary, for example, people who come to give you work or ask you for something interrupt what you are doing, and interruptions become part of the normal working life. If people approach you and wait for you to turn to them and give them your full attention they are not normally a problem.

The people who are a problem are those who burst in and blatantly interrupt what you are doing, without so much as a by your leave, or are continually butting in when you are trying to say something to them, or to somebody else.

The same thing applies whether you are speaking face-to-face or on the 'phone. How do you deal with people who butt in? They are ill-mannered, but that is no reason for you to be ill-mannered in return, so it does no good to say 'Oh, shut up!', unless you know them very well indeed, and can get away with it. You certainly could not say that sort of thing to your boss or to someone whom you meet only occasionally in a business environment. You would never say it to an external customer, so do not say it to an internal customer.

So what do you do?

1 If you are on the 'phone and somebody, no matter who it is, bursts in and interrupts your conversation, you cannot concentrate on two things at once so:
   - say 'Excuse me a moment' to the person on the 'phone
   - turn to the interrupter and say 'Excuse me, I'll be with you as soon as I can'
   - turn back to the 'phone and finish the call as quickly as possible; offer to ring back if necessary

- turn to the interrupter and ask how you can help, without being
  sarcastic about it.

In other words, acknowledge both parties and deal with them in turn;
just waving a hand at the interrupter is not usually good enough.

2 If you are talking to someone in the room and someone else bursts in
   and interrupts your conversation, it depends whether you are the
   senior or the junior of the two holding the conversation. (Assume that
   the conversation is important, and not just chat.)
   - If you are the junior, allow the other person to deal with the
     interrupter
   - If you are the senior, do exactly as you would if you were on the
     telephone – that is, acknowledge both and deal with both in turn.

If the interrupter has burst in at a very awkward moment take time
later to point out that the interruption made the situation difficult for
you. You are telling the other person off, but doing it in such a way
that you are saying that you were put out, rather than saying that they
were in the wrong. This is useful if you are junior to the interrupter. If
you are senior, you can tell them they were out of order to come
bursting in, but do it later, not in front of the person with whom you
were having the original conversation. If the interrupter apologises,
accept the apology, and say no more about it.

In addition, there are two things you can do to prevent the same
interrupter doing the same thing again:
- make sure that you never interrupt them in that way: behaviour
  breeds behaviour
- let it be known to the switchboard and everyone else that you are
  having an important meeting and **no** interruptions are permitted.

Some companies have a very formal method of doing this. Solicitors,
for example, might have a red warning light on the outside of the door
which lights up when they are with a client. In some open-plan offices
people have a little red 'flag' they can display on the desk when they
particularly do not want to be interrupted – when they are writing
something which needs extra concentration, or keying in something
very urgent, or about to make a difficult 'phone call. This works well
provided that everyone abides by the rules, and no-one abuses the red
flag system.

3 If you are trying to talk to someone who is continually butting in and
   not letting you finish your sentences:
   - stop talking
   - wait until they stop
   - start again at the original point without saying 'As I was saying'. If
     you say 'As I was saying', you are, in effect, telling them off and

saying 'As I was saying when I was so rudely interrupted'.
If you try to 'talk over' them – that is, get your point across in a louder voice – you will both be talking at once, neither able to hear what the other is saying. If you wait long enough, they will eventually stop talking.

Sometimes you know someone well enough to say in a calm voice 'Did you know you butted in just then?' If so, fine, but only use it to your own peer group, the people you work with regularly who are on the same level as you.

 ## Compulsive talkers – face-to-face and on the 'phone

Compulsive talkers are the sort of people who do not listen, have lots to say and go on and on, or just drop in for a chat and are difficult to get rid of. Sometimes it does not matter if people keep rabbiting on, but sometimes it does, because you need to get your point across or get on with your work.

First, the people who keep talking and will not listen, perhaps sometimes because they do not want to hear – how can you deal with them? There are two main things you can do:
- wait until they take a breath or come to a natural pause, then leap in very quickly and bring them firmly back to the point you wanted to discuss. You might have to do this two or three times.
- say their name over and over again, getting louder as you do so – mr smith . . . Mr Smith . . . MR SMITH, until in the end they say 'Well, what?!' Then you can say what you have to. This works very well on the 'phone.

Now what about the people who come to chat while you are trying to work?
- stop what you are doing
- turn your whole body towards them, giving them your full attention
- ask what they want

If they want something they will tell you. If they want nothing, there is nothing more that they can say. If they say they just stopped by for a chat, you can point out that you are very busy just now, but you will meet them later. This is a WIN/WIN situation all the way.

People who do not speak good English – face-to-face and on the 'phone

There are many reasons for not speaking or understanding English well. People might be from a different part of the world, or have lived in the UK for some time but still speak very little English. They might find it difficult to understand your accent, and you theirs. Communication on the telephone between, say, someone from Aberdeen and someone from Birmingham can be quite a problem.

Here is a list of things to do when you are trying to communicate face-to-face with someone who finds you hard to understand:
- stand or sit looking directly at them
- don't shout
- speak slowly and distinctly, separating the words
- smile
- use gestures to demonstrate
- watch their eyes for understanding
- use simple language, not slang or jargon
- say things in a different way, if necessary
- have patience
- watch them for gestures
- listen and don't interrupt
- check your understanding by asking limiting or closed questions (see Chapter 2)
- encourage them to keep talking by nodding and smiling
- don't correct their English unnecessarily: as long as you understand what they want, that is all that matters. Correcting pronunciation or grammar is a bit of a put down.

On the telephone it is much more difficult, because you have not got the body language signals to pick up and the telephone tends to distort voices anyway. There is also the difficulty of the slight time lapse if you are speaking to someone on the other side of the world, and your voices are bouncing off a satellite.

In these circumstances, try this:

1 Make sure the line is clear: get as clean a line as possible; if it is really crackly, try to get re-connected.

2 Check your own understanding: repeat back, slowly, anything important the other person says.

3 Speak clearly: speak slowly and distinctly, making each word very

58

clear. For example, say 'please – can – you – send – me – a – fax', rather than 'pleasecanyousendmeafax' all run together. Say the little words like 'a' and 'the' clearly; we tend to swallow them.

4 Use simple language: use standard words and phrases, the sort of words that people would learn as they learn English. For example, they would probably understand 'the computer is not working' but they might not know the phrase 'the computer has gone down'. Do not use words which are special to your part of the country, if you can help it. For example, 'I can't wait while Wednesday' instead of 'I can't wait until Wednesday' might baffle people who live in other parts of the world, or other parts of the UK.

5 Check names: if you cannot understand their name, ask them to spell it, and then spell it back to them. You might have to do this several times, which is embarrassing, but it is better than getting it wrong.

   Patience, perseverance and an understanding that people do not have to speak good English will help you communicate with them. Admire them for trying, and be as helpful as possible.

 ## People who don't want to know

People who don't want to know at work are usually internal customers. They are the people who will not listen, do not want help, do the minimum amount of work to get by and are generally a pain to work with, whether they are senior to you, junior to you or on your level.
   These people are really difficult to work with, so what can you do about them?

1 You can try to ignore them if that is what they want and you feel comfortable about it. It is not always possible to do this anyway, because sometimes you need their cooperation to do your own job properly.

2 You can try to find out what does interest them – there must be something in this world they like to do or talk about, unless they are ill, depressed or on drugs. If you can begin to talk to them about what interests them outside work and ask questions about it, they might at last begin to cooperate with you inside work. You might become the person they do not mind talking to and working with.

3 If they are ill, depressed or on drugs, it depends what their relationship is to you. If you are junior to them, there is little you can do except try to understand and be as helpful as possible. If you are their direct line manager, you have to talk with them about their illness, and between you see what can be done about it; you cannot let it slide by unnoticed. If they are on your level, try sympathy and asking what you can do to help.

People who don't want to know often have a personal problem of some sort. It is not up to you to pry, but if you can become aware of the problem at least you will have a better understanding of what makes that person tick. Some people do not respond whatever you try; you just have to learn to live and work with them as they are.

 ## People who have disabilities

People are disabled in many different ways, and the mistake that others often make is to treat them all in exactly the same way. As a general rule, people have these disabilities: they
- are deaf or hard of hearing
- are blind or partially sighted
- are wheelchair bound for physical reasons only
- are wheelchair bound and unable to coordinate their limbs, but their brain is otherwise normal
- are mentally disabled or ill
- have diseases such as epilepsy
- are slow of thought and speech because of age, disease or illness

A well-known Radio 4 programme is called *Does he take sugar?* It is a programme for and about people with disabilities, and it got its name through someone who could not recognise that people in wheelchairs are not necessarily brain-damaged. When handing round the tea the person asked the wheelchair man's companion 'Does he take sugar?' instead of talking to the wheelchair man direct.

People with a disability sometimes, but not always, need your help at work, whether they are internal or external customers. It is impossible here to write down all the things they might or might not need from you, so here is a list of very general DOs and DON'Ts

If you are dealing with someone with a disability:

DO
- get to know the person
- get to know the limits their disability places on them

60

- help when asked or when you know it is needed
- speak slowly and clearly for deaf and hard-of-hearing people
- look at people to check their understanding
- remember that blind or partially-sighted people need you to describe things to them

DON'T
- assume that people in wheelchairs are stupid
- stare at them, even if they are deaf; speaking clearly is more important
- insist on helping when help is not needed
- talk down to people in wheelchairs; put yourself on their level
- be afraid of them
- ignore them

As we have said all through this chapter, think of people as people with difficulties or disabilities rather than difficult or disabled people; think of people as people, and it will help you to know how to deal with them.

 People who are timid

Timid people are usually shy, lacking in self-confidence, quietly spoken and a bit withdrawn; they do not look directly at you. The difficulty with timid people is that it is very often a great problem to find out what they can do, what they know and what they think about things. They often have very good ideas and work hard and well, so it is a mistake to underestimate them, but an easy thing to do.

Some timid people are quite happy to remain in the background, which is fine as long as they do their work well. If this is the case, do not make the mistake of forcing them to join in, or putting them in a position where they have to show confidence and be outgoing. If someone is happy buried in a computer, do not make them a salesperson or a trainer.

What about people who are timid, but want to gain in self-confidence and join fully in every aspect of working life? They need praise for what they do well, they need encouragement to try new things and they need to **know** that people will not laugh at them if they do something wrong. What they can do without is people telling them not to be shy or people being scornful at the way they do things. They need the positives, not the negatives: everyone needs positives rather than negatives, but timid people need them more than most.

Here are a few things you can do to help timid people and make them easier to work with:

- Don't give them things to do which they are unlikely to achieve
- Don't laugh at them if they get things wrong
- Praise them a lot
- Encourage them to try new things
- Thank them for their help, and let them know how valuable it is
- Don't ignore them, but don't drag them into the limelight if they don't want to be there

Treat them as people with a difficulty.

	Practice

1 Look back over this chapter.
2 Write down a list of people with whom you come into regular contact who you find difficult. It might be a list of only one. You can put down specific people, or types of people – for example, 'people who shout at me'. Make sure you write down where the difficulty lies.
3 Choose one, or at the most two, of the people on your list.
4 Try to analyse what you find so difficult about those people. For example, 'she shouts at me so I can't think straight' or 'I never know whether Mike wants a hand getting his wheelchair through the door or not'.
5 Write down what **you** are going to do about your chosen people with difficulties. For example, 'Next time Jill shouts at me I will keep calm, wait until she has finished shouting and ask her to show me how to do it properly, because I want to get it right' or 'I'll ask Mike whether he wants help with the door, and what help he does or doesn't want'.
6 Do whatever you have written down.

	Points to remember in this chapter

- People are people with difficulties, not difficult people
- Behaviour breeds behaviour
- Let angry people run out of steam: listen and don't interrupt
- Silence can be powerful
- If people are aggressive, follow the rules and get help
- Agree with your colleagues how much verbal abuse is acceptable
- If people interrupt, deal with one thing and one person at a time
- Compulsive talkers have to breathe some time
- Speak clearly and listen hard to understand and be understood
- People who don't want to know often have a personal problem – which is not you
- There are many disabilities; don't treat them all the same
- Timid people need the positives, not the negatives

Further reading

Face-to-face communication
Vera Hughes and David Weller, *Self Presentation Skills* (Macmillan, 1991), Chapter 6.

6 | People Who are in Distress

In this chapter:
- External customers
  - stressful situations
  - what to do
  - what not to do
- Internal customers
  - stressful situations
  - what to do
  - what not to do
- Your own needs

External and internal 'customers' are treated separately in this chapter because you need to look at their stressful situations and what you can do from a different standpoint. External customers will look to you for professional help; they will view you as the one who knows what to do, and is in charge. This might be so for internal customers, but not necessarily.

 ## External customers in stressful situations

A stressful situation can vary from someone who comes into a shop with a complaint to someone contacting an insurance company to let them know that their husband or wife has died or has had a very bad car crash.

Take an example somewhere between the two extremes:

Ernest Williams has had a minor car accident, but is really upset about it because it is a brand new car and he has been driving for many years and has never had to make a claim before.

| | *Exercise 1* |

Read the following telephone conversation between Mr Williams and Miss Janet Hodgson who works in the Claims Department of an insurance company. You are looking for:

(a) what Janet Hodgson did right
(b) what she could have done better.

If you are working in a group or in pairs, one of you could read the part of Mr Williams and another the part of Janet as a role play.

Janet: Good morning, Claims Department. Janet Hodgson speaking.
Mr W: Oh, good morning.
Janet: How may I help you?
Mr W: Well, I backed into the gate post in my new car, you see, and I thought I had better let you know about it. It's quite a nasty bump, I'm afraid.
Janet: Yes, sir, quite right. May I take down a few details and then I can let you have a claim form.
Mr W: Oh, yes. Well, You see I was reversing down the drive, and this car is a bit bigger than my old one. It's such a shame – a brand new car. I don't know what my wife is going to say about it.
Janet: No, sir. I didn't mean the details of the accident. I meant your name, policy number, vehicle registration number and that sort of detail.
Mr W: My policy number? I've no idea. My wife puts these things away in a drawer, you see, and she deals with all that sort of thing. Goodness knows what she's going to say about all this. I've never had to make a claim before, you see.
Janet: Never mind about the policy number just now, sir. If you could just give me your name, please.
Mr W: My name? Oh! It's Williams, Ernest Williams.
Janet: Thank you. And your address?
Mr W: It's 21 Lakeside Way, Carlisle.
Janet: 21 Lakeside Way, Carlisle. And the postcode Mr Williams?
Mr W: Oh, dear. I can't ever remember the postcode. Do you really need it? My wife will know it, but she's out at the moment.
Janet: We do need the postcode if possible, because that's part of the coding system on our VDUs, but never mind. Have you got comprehensive insurance, Mr Williams?
Mr W: Oh, yes. I think so.
Janet: That's OK then. If you had only got third party, fire and theft,

you wouldn't be able to claim for this.

Mr W: Well, I'm pretty sure we have, but I'll have to check with my wife when she comes back. I hope she won't be long.

Janet: And the vehicle registration number?

Mr W: Um . . . J181 KGW, I think. Or is it KWG? It's a new car, you see . . .

Janet: J181 KGW, thank you.

Mr W: Is there anything else you need to know?

Janet: No, no, that's all thanks. I'll put the claim form in the post for you today. Thank you Mr Williams. Goodbye.

Mr W: Oh, goodbye. (*Puts 'phone down*) (*To himself*) Perhaps I'd better go and move the car before Winnie gets home. Don't want her to see it stuck in the driveway until I've explained. Now what did I do with the keys . . . ?

Write down:

(a) The things Janet did well: for example she answered the 'phone properly when she first picked up the receiver.

(b) The things she could have done better, or need not have said at all: for example, she could have asked for the customer's name much earlier, and asked for it very directly, which would have prevented all the rigmarole about reversing down the drive etc.

You can assume that she knows her job and that what she says about the coding system and the insurance policy is right.

When you have made your list, compare it with the list below.

(a) What Janet did well

1 She answered the 'phone properly, saying greeting, department and her own name.

2 She knew her job and what she needed to process the claim. She knew that the postcode would be helpful but not essential, and she did not press Mr Williams about it.

3 She knew that she must try to check whether the car was comprehensively insured or not.

4 She used Mr Williams' name as soon as she could, but called him 'sir' until she knew his name.

5 She did not insist on being told the policy number when she realised it would be difficult for Mr Williams to find it.

6 She tried to reassure Mr Williams – for example, saying 'Never mind about the policy number' and 'that's OK then'.

7 She seemed to be patient and did not make any unkind remarks like 'I'd love to see your wife's face when she gets home!'

(b) What Janet could have done better

1 She could have said she was sorry to hear about the 'nasty bump' right at the start, and sympathised that it was a new car. Accident claims are all in a day's work to her, but for Mr Williams it was a small tragedy.

2 It is unwise to rattle off all sorts of things you need to know all at once – 'I meant your name, policy number, vehicle registration number and that sort of detail' she said. When people are in distress they cannot think clearly and quickly, so you need to take things a step at a time, and often fairly slowly.

3 Janet could have reassured Mr Williams even further when he said he had never had to make a claim before. She deals with several every day, but it is the first time for him.

4 It is helpful sometimes to let people know why you want information – 'it's part of the coding system' – but she need not have used jargon terms – 'on our VDUs'.

5 Having established that Mr Williams was comprehensively insured (he seemed fairly certain about that) there was no need to say what would have happened if he had not. Do not confuse people who are in distress. Stick to the simple facts.

6 She did not seem to pick up Mr Williams' uncertainy about the vehicle registration number. There could be problems there later. Persevere and get the facts right.

7 She made no mention of Mrs Williams at all; if Mrs Williams is the one who looks after the household administration, which seems likely, Janet could have suggested that Mrs Williams ring her later in the day; she would need to leave her name, telephone number and extension with Mr Williams. When people are in distress it is a good idea to give them something definite to do – something fairly simple which you know they can do. This is part of the difference between sympathy and empathy (see Chapter 11).

In the conversation between Janet and Mr Williams, we were not able to hear her tone of voice; when you are dealing with people in distress your voice should sound calm, matter-of-fact, friendly and, if necessary, a little authoritative. People are coming to you for your professional advice and help, and they often want and need to be told what to do. This does not mean that you cannot say words of sympathy, but it does mean that you need to sound as though you know what you are talking about.

If you are dealing with someone face-to-face your body language, too, needs to be positive, but not too hurried. Look your customer in the eye so that your eyes show understanding, but if the other person gets very distressed, remember to look away for a while so that they have time to recover. A friendly hand on the arm or shoulder is sometimes welcome, but not always; you have to judge the situation.

Here is a list of the possible types of situation where your external customers might be in distress and looking for professional help. This is followed by a general list of DOs and DON'Ts which apply in most situations.

Stressful situations
- making a complaint
- after an accident of any sort
- when people owe money and cannot pay
- in a situation new to them
- when something or somebody is lost
- after a death
- recently separated or divorced

DO
- listen
- show sympathy
- know your product/service
- be patient
- ask for facts clearly, one at a time
- contact another person, if appropriate
- give the customer something definite to do
- sound and look professional
- reassure people

DON'T
- treat people in distress as if it is just a job to you
- go too fast
- laugh, even if it strikes you as funny
- use complicated English or jargon
- confuse people with unnecessary questions or information
- panic!

 Internal customers in stressful situations

Many of the same DOs and DON'Ts apply when you are dealing with people inside your organisation who are in distress, but the situations are likely to be different.

68

Exercise 2

Take each type of situation mentioned below and make a list, with your neighbour or by yourself, of the DOs and DON'Ts you would apply to it.

For example, the situation is that people can become very pressurised at work, with an enormous workload. If you were working with a colleague in this sort of situation, what would you do and not do?

1 Colleague is very overworked
   DO
   • let them get on with it
   DON'T
   • try to chat

Complete the list of DOs and DON'Ts for this situation, and then do the same for these situations.

2 Colleague has just been told off with good reason
3 Vital equipment has just broken down
4 Colleague suffers from permanent disability or illness
5 Person is new to organisation
6 Colleague has a bad cold
7 Colleague has recently received personal bad news
8 Someone junior has made a bad mistake, and realises it

Check what you have written against these lists, which have probably left out things you have written and put in things which you have not written. Your lists and these together will make good guidelines for dealing with internal customers in distress.

1 Colleague is very overworked
   DO
   • notice they are under pressure
   • offer to help if possible, particularly with small, basic jobs
   • let them get on with their work
   • fetch cups of tea/coffee to help them through
   • find something to do yourself, rather than doing nothing
   • congratulate them when they've got through it all
   DON'T
   • try to chat

- interrupt
- make unhelpful remarks about their management of time

2 Colleague has just been told off with good reason
DO
- listen, if they want to tell you about it
- show your support and sympathy
- offer to help so it won't happen again
- give the person something to do that you know they can do well, or ask for their help

DON'T
- pry
- indulge in a hate session against the teller off
- be prejudiced against the teller off yourself

3 Vital equipment has just broken down
DO
- offer to 'phone the engineer
- suggest alternative ways of dealing with the work
- suggest they re-negotiate deadlines
  (see Chapter 4)
- take charge, if necessary

DON'T
- laugh
- panic
- try to mend or unjam equipment you don't know

4 Colleague suffers from permanent disability or illness
(see Chapter 5)
DO
- find out the limits their disability places on them (what they can and can't do)
- help when asked, or when you know it is needed
- keep working as normal yourself
- treat them as normally as possible

DON'T
- insist on helping if help is not needed
- go overboard with sympathy
- give them all the easy or boring jobs to do
- give them jobs they cannot do

5 Person is new to organisation
DO
- make them welcome

- show them what they need to know – a bit at a time
- introduce them to other people – as they need to know
- make sure they know where tools, equipment, stationery etc are
- make sure they have something to do as soon as possible
- tell them who to turn to for help

DON'T
- ignore them
- assume they know anything – check
- assume they know nothing – check
- throw them in at the deep end

5 Colleague has a bad cold
DO
- sympathise
- understand if they are a bit slower than usual
- keep working as normal
- do a bit extra, without making a song and dance about it

DON'T
- make too much of it
- get too close!
- insist they take your cold remedies if they don't want them

7 Colleague has recently received personal bad news
DO
- be aware something is wrong
- listen, if they want to talk
- let them have time to themselves, if necessary
- do a bit extra to lighten the load for them
- keep working as normal
- give them time to sort things out, if necessary
- let them know you are sorry

DON'T
- pry
- keep talking about it, if they don't want to
- keep on saying 'are you all right?'
- be afraid to talk about it, if they want to
- smother them with sympathy

8 Someone junior has just made a bad mistake, and realises it
DO
- accept their apology
- say you won't expect it to happen again; take disciplinary action if necessary

- offer to give them help or training or whatever is needed to put the matter right
- take responsibility for the mistake, if necessary

DON'T

- go on and on about it
- shout at them
- tell everybody else
- tell them they are no good
- take them off the job unless absolutely necessary

Your own needs

If you have been dealing with people in distress or in stressful situations, you will be affected by it yourself to a greater or lesser degree. You need to recognise this and do whatever is necessary to be able to work calmly and well again. The situation is similar to when you have to deal with aggressive or abusive people, as described in Chapter 5.

Different people do different things to recover from stressful situations. Some people do not appear to be affected by stress at all, and just let everything wash over them. If you are not one of those people, and find yourself unable to concentrate or keep thinking about what has happened, give yourself time to do whatever you have to do to recover. Usually something fairly active helps, but there are limits to what you can do at work.

Here are some ideas; see if you can add to them:

- take a break, and have a wash and brush up
- have a cup of tea or coffee
- excuse yourself, and go for a walk round the block for ten minutes
- do an easy job which does not require a lot of thought
- tell someone about it

If your whole job is stressful, like working in a credit control department where you might be on the 'phone all day chasing up money owed to the company, you will find it very difficult to work all day without quite a few breaks. This does not mean taking a fifteen-minute tea break every twenty minutes; it does mean pacing yourself so that you can spend a certain amount of time making the difficult 'phone calls, but you intersperse those calls with other, easier tasks.

Dealing with people who in distress can really take it out of you, so know how to deal with yourself as well.

72

┌─────────┬──┐

Points to remember in this chapter

- What is stressful to one person is not necessarily so to another
- An everyday job to you might be new and stressful for others
- People in distress want help and look to you to give it in a professional way
- Let people know you sympathise and are sorry they are in distress
- Take charge, if necessary
- People in distress often think and act more slowly
- Your tone of voice must be calm and sometimes authoritative
- Keep things as normal as possible
- Offer help where it is needed, don't wait to be asked
- Get distressed people to do something specific
- Know how to deal with yourself

7 Complaints

In this chapter:
- Making complaints
  - when to complain
  - to whom to complain
  - how to complain
  - agreeing the outcome
- Dealing with complaints
  - from external customers
  - from internal customers

Making complaints

How good are you at making complaints? When you have bought
something which is not quite right, do you take it back to the shop, or do
you just let it go? It takes a lot of courage for some people to complain,
but if goods are faulty or services are not adequate we should do so.

Complaining does not mean going in or writing in an aggressive
manner, or whingeing about something; it means putting across the
facts and sorting out with the people who have supplied the faulty
goods or services what to do about it. If you approach people well when
you want to make a complaint, they are usually very helpful and
anxious to please.

When to complain

Sometimes it is difficult to know whether you should complain or not,
perhaps because you have had the goods for some time. There are
several questions you can ask yourself to help you decide whether to
complain or not.

Ask yourself:

1 About something you have bought:
- is it new and does not work?
- has it been used for quite a while, but then starts going wrong when it should be still OK (for example, a really expensive piece of furniture which starts to fall apart after about eighteen months)?
- is it fit for the purpose for which it was intended? This one is a bit legalistic, but there is a term called 'merchantable quality'; this means that anything sold must be fit for the purpose for which it was made. A good example here is a thin bedroom carpet which was sold to you as a kitchen carpet; you put it in the kitchen and of course it wears out in no time. You would have to prove to the retailer, or your local Office of Fair Trading, that it **was** sold to you as a kitchen carpet, which might be difficult.

If you can answer 'yes' to any or some of these questions you should take the item back and make a complaint about it.

2 About a service you have paid for, like a holiday, or a visit to the hairdresser:
- did I get full value for money?
- was everything done that was promised?
- did I miss anything in the small print?

If you can honestly answer 'no' to any of these questions you should consider making a complaint. It is more difficult to prove that things were not right when you have received a service, so you need to be very specific about what was wrong. For example, you need to be able to say exactly how long a flight was delayed, how often your room was without hot water and that sort of thing. Being vague will not help your cause. You need to have read all the small print very carefully, too.

3 About someone's treatment of you:
- what did the person actually say?
- what did the person actually do?
- what did the person not do that s/he should have done?

It is even more difficult to prove that someone has treated you badly, particularly if you have been involved in an argument. If you want to make a complaint about someone (it could be someone at work, or someone like a sales assistant or a waiter), you have to be able to say accurately what was said and done. Write it all down as soon as you possibly can after the event to help you remember; this might seem a bit cold and calculating, but memory plays tricks and a few notes jotted down will help you a lot.

To whom to complain

The person to whom to complain is someone who can do something about it. Complain to the decision maker: there is always someone, somewhere who can make a decision.

The usual thing to do is to go back to the shop where you bought the goods or the people who arranged the service for you (the travel agent, for example). If the complaint is not a very major one, people at that level usually have the authority to do something about putting the matter right.

If it is something major, persevere until you are given the name, or at least the job title, of the person who can deal fully with your complaint.

If you are writing, try to write to a named person; you can often find out a person's name by ringing a company and saying you want to write to the sales manager, or the customer services manager and could you have his or her name, please. If you cannot get a name, write to a job title like The Sales Manager or The Personnel Manager or The Chairman. If you write to a company (for example, you address your letter to Supergroup plc) addressing them as 'Dear Sirs', your letter is likely to wander from department to department without finding anyone to reply to it, so write to a definite person or job title. One problem about writing to The Chairman is that the letter is normally acknowledged and passed down the line to someone who can actually do something about the matter; however, the head of a company does not like receiving complaints letters, and will often make sure that something is done by somebody else, so for a serious complaint it is worth going to the top.

When you are at work, and you feel you must make a complaint about the way you have been treated or something serious is wrong, there is usually a Grievance Procedure to follow, particularly in medium and big companies. The procedure is normally written down in your company handbook or sometimes in your Contract of Employment letter. In some serious cases you can consider going to your Trade Union Representative. Whatever the procedure is, you should follow it. It usually says that you should go to your direct line manager or supervisor first, and if you get no satisfaction, take your complaint up the line.

If it is a trivial matter you have to complain about, do something about it rather than whingeing about it to your friends. It will help to make the working atmosphere much better if you say what is wrong, provided you have good reason to complain. However, life can be very uncomfortable at work if you get the reputation of somebody who is always complaining, so you need to be sure of your ground.

How to complain

Act like a reasonable human being and your complaint is much more
likely to be dealt with properly. This means:
- Collect your facts
- State the facts clearly and reasonably
- Say what you want done
    Let us look at each of these separately.

- *Collect your facts*
When you are complaining about goods you have bought, the sort of
facts you need are:
    - proof of purchase (receipt, till slip etc)
    - when you bought the item
    - when it was first used
    - how often it has been used
    - exactly what is wrong with it
For goods you have sent for which have not been delivered:
    - date of order
    - cheque or Postal Order number
    - exactly what was ordered
    - where you saw the item advertised
For services you have received which are unsatisfactory:
    - what you expected
    - what you paid, and proof of payment, if appropriate
    - exactly what happened which was wrong
    - what did not happen which should have
    - any backup documents (eg an airline flight delay card)
If you have been badly treated at work:
    - when it happened
    - how often it happened
    - exactly what happened
    - what was said to you
    - what you said to other people
    - who can back you up in what you say
    Collect as many facts as you can, and have any backup documents
readily available.

- *State the facts clearly and reasonably*
If you have got to the stage of making a complaint, particularly if it is at
work, you are probably pretty wound up and angry or really upset.
Sometimes you cannot help showing this, which is understandable, but
do not let emotion muddle the facts.
    If people are really angry and start shouting they often say things

they do not mean, or exaggerate things or get things out of proportion. If you are in this state when you are making a complaint, other people will perhaps get angry themselves until neither of you can see the facts clearly. Be as calm and clear as you can, and certainly not aggressive.

If you are **writing** to complain about something there is no reason at all to use emotive language. You can write that you are distressed or disappointed, or even angry, but phrases such as 'I think your company should be banned' or 'Your service is the pits' are not very likely to help get the matter sorted out!

If the complaint has got to a very serious stage, and nothing you can say or do seems to get things moving, you can eventually say that you will go to your Solicitor or the court unless something is done; if you get to that stage, be prepared to do what you say and do it promptly. There is no point in making idle threats or hanging it out.

At work try to pick a time and a place when the person to whom you are complaining can listen to you. People who are very pushed for time or talking to someone else or in the middle of a long and complicated job will not be able to give you their full attention. Ask if the time is convenient, and if necessary come back when it is more suitable.

In Chapter 5 we were thinking about dealing with people with difficulties and getting to a WIN/WIN situation. When you complain you are a person with a difficulty, so do all you can to help towards a WIN/WIN situation for you both.

- *Say what you want done*

Be clear in your own mind before you make a complaint what you want done about the matter; these are the sorts of outcomes you might be looking for:
- your money back
- items exchanged
- compensation
- something off the next purchase
- the item repaired free of charge
- a part replaced
- something re-done
- equipment mended
- more overtime
- less overtime
- equipment replaced
- work given to you earlier
- better handwriting
- clearer instructions
- an apology
- people to stop doing something

- people to start doing something

There are all sorts of things you could want in various circumstances, so know what you are aiming to get out of making your complaint. If you are clear about this, and are able to say what you want, it will stop you complaining for the sake of it.

Agreeing the outcome

This is where some negotiation comes in. You know what you want, and have said so, verbally or in writing, but in your heart of hearts you know that you are unlikely to get it all, so there are two more things you need to know before you make a complaint:

- what you must have (your bottom line)
- what you will accept

For example, you have taken a raincoat to the cleaners, you get just outside the door and realise that the belt is missing. You do all the right things – go back into the shop, explain the facts, show them the raincoat still in its plastic cover and say that you want the belt found, please. This is what you want, but it might not be possible to do this, so what must you have, and what will you accept? You might decide that you must have compensation of some sort and that you cannot possibly accept the situation as it is, but you will accept some money to buy a new belt or a certain amount off your next cleaning bill.

At work, for example, you might have decided to complain to your supervisor that the photocopier is always breaking down and preventing you from getting papers out on time. Again you have done all the right things; you have:

- collected all the facts (perhaps written down how many times it has gone wrong in a week and how long it took to get the engineer in)
- gone to the right person
- chosen the right moment
- said you want a new photocopier

You realise that you will probably not get a new copier, but you can decide that you **must have** something more reliable and **can accept** a newer model, or a faster call-out time for the engineer or a different system so that not so many people use it. You might not get all you want, but at least you will have improved matters and you will both be in a WIN/WIN situation. If you want more detail about how to conduct this sort of negotiation, read Chapter 7 of *Self Presentation Skills*.

The important thing here is that you both know and agree what the outcome of the complaint is to be. The person to whom you are complaining will also know what they want, what they must have and what they will accept – this is all part of the skill of negotiation. With flexibility and goodwill on both sides you can probably reach a WIN/WIN situation.

Exercise 1

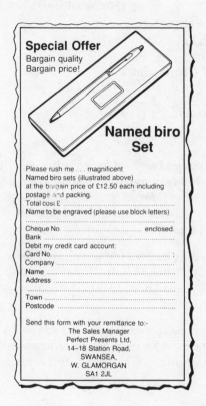

You recently sent off for a named biro set as a birthday present for your mother, whose name is Margaret. You saw this ad in your local newspaper and filled in the form, wrote out your Building Society cheque no 0010243 and sent it 1st class. That was four weeks ago and you have not heard. Your mother's birthday is only ten days away and you are getting worried about her present.

Write to the mail order company complaining about the delay and saying what you want done. Make up the date of the cheque (pages 76–78 should help you).

Write the letter without looking at this example, and then compare your letter with what is written here.

1 (Date)   **2** (Home address)

3 The Sales Manager
Perfect Presents Ltd
14–16 Station Road
SWANSEA   W Glamorgan
SA1 2JL

4 Dear Sales Manager

5 *NAMED BIRO SET*

6 About four weeks ago I sent off for your Biro Birthday set for my mother's birthday. **7** I saw your advertisement in the Swansea Echo and posted off the Order Form, first class, with my cheque. **8** The cheque number is 0010243 and it was dated (date of cheque). **9** My mother's name is Margaret.

10 I am worried that the biro set has not arrived, because my mother's birthday is in ten days' time. **11** If the present does not arrive before (state a definite date) I shall have to cancel the order and think of something else to give her.

12 Please would you make sure the biro set arrives by (date stated) or return my cheque to me. **13** If there is any difficulty, please telephone me *at work*; my work number is (work no, and extension if applicable).

14 Yours faithfully
15 (signature)
16 (NAME IN BLOCK CAPITALS)

Notes:
1 Always date your letters
2 Give the same address as the address on the Order Form
3 You do not know the name of the person dealing with these orders, so use a job title
4 You do not know whether the Sales Manager is a man or a woman, so you can use the job title
5 Put a heading, so the person receiving the letter knows immediately what it is about
6 Write down the facts – clearly
7 Say where you saw the ad: it might help to pinpoint your order. If you can send a photocopy of your order, so much the better

8 Give the cheque no and date
9 Could be helpful information
10 Say why you are writing and why it is urgent
11 Say what you are going to to
12 Say what you want the company to do
13 Only say this if you can be contacted at work. A telephone or fax number is often useful
14 'Yours faithfully' is the normal signatory when you have not used a person's name in the salutation (Dear . . .)
15 Remember to sign the letter
16 Write your name clearly so that it can be easily read. If you are a woman add Mrs, Miss or Ms; otherwise they might assume you are a man.

Dealing with complaints from external customers

You may or may not have to deal with complaints from external customers in your work; it will depend on your job and what your status is within the company. If you are fairly new to the job you will probably not be allowed to deal with complaints; you will have to pass the person on to a manager. However, the customer has come to you, and you need to be seen to deal with the person, even if you cannot deal with the actual complaint.

The sequence runs like this:
- Greet the customer (you would do this anyway)
- Listen

If you are dealing with the complaint yourself:
- Sort out the facts – is the complaint justified?
- Apologise if necessary
- Say what you will do to put the matter right

We will look at each point from 'Listen' onwards separately.

- *Listen*

People who have a complaint to make need someone to listen to them. You practised your listening skills in Chapter 2, and this is a situation where you will need to put all these skills to good use.

Even if you are not going to deal with the complaint yourself, you need to listen to the complainer and show with your body language that you are listening. When the complainer has explained the main cause of complaint, say that you will ask your manager to deal with the customer before he or she goes into too much detail. Try to get the complainer's name and the main points of the complaint so that you can pass these on to your manager.

Look or sound (on the 'phone) as if you know what you are doing. If you say 'Oh I don't know, I'm new here' the customer will not feel confident that the complaint will be properly handled.

If you are going to deal with the complaint yourself you can go on to the next stage.

- *Sort out the facts – is the complaint justified?*

People who complain are often a bit wound up and sometimes aggressive (see Chapter 5). By questioning and responding, as you practised in Chapter 2, you can cool the situation down and get at the real facts of the complaint in a calm and adult sort of way. Take as long as you need to over this stage.

- *Apologise if necessary*

If the company is at fault, apologise. Just say you are sorry and leave it at that. There is nothing to be gained by going on the defensive and explaining to the customer why something did not happen or why something was late. Customers do not want to know your problems – they want their complaint dealt with.

Do not blame other people in the company. It is very, very easy to do this without knowing you are doing it. You say things like 'Oh, I'm sorry, Head Office must have . . .' or 'I wasn't here then and so-and-so dealt with it'.

Customers do not want to know who is to blame, and blaming others does not show very good teamwork (see Chapter 8). You are the company's representative at that moment, so apologise on behalf of the company, and get the customer's mind off what went wrong.

- *Say what you will do to put the matter right*

Be definite about what is to happen next. The situation might require some negotiation, as we saw earlier in this chapter, and the final outcome might be decided at this point. Make sure that you and the complainer know what the next step is to be and agree upon it.

If there is nothing you can do (if the complaint is unjustified) be firm about it. Do not make promises you know you will not be able to keep, and do not make promises for other people: you have no way of guaranteeing that other people will keep promises made on their behalf.

Exercise 2

This is an exercise in complaining, in dealing with a complaint and learning from watching others.

Do the exercise in threes: one complainer, one listener and one observer. The threes can all do this simultaneously, so that there are several goups of three working at the same time in the same room. Complainers can look at pages 73–78 to help them prepare. Listeners can use pages 81 and 82 and Chapter 2.

1 Decide who is to play which role.

2 Decide what the complaint is to be about; it should be about something familiar to both complainer and listener so that a sensible conversation can take place. The observer needs to know the subject. Try to make the complaint a fairly substantial one which will take a little time to sort out.

3 Arrange tables and chairs to resemble the situation as it would be – for example, across a counter, standing up; across a desk, sitting down; standing or sitting without a barrier between you.

4 Observers should be able to see and hear the other two in their group, but not be close enough to be in the way. Observers can use the list below to help them; jot things down as you see and hear them.

5 The listener must deal with the complaint – not pass it on to someone else!

6 Complainer and listener practise complaining and listening.

WHEN IT IS FINISHED

7 Discuss among the three of you what went on, in this order:
   7.1 Complainer says how s/he felt and how well the complaint was dealt with
   7.2 Listener says how s/he felt and how well the complaint was made
   7.3 Observer says what s/he saw and heard.
   If you wish you can do this three times, swapping roles each time, or you can do it twice and leave the third one until you have read the section about handling complaints from internal customers.

MAKING A COMPLAINT – OBSERVER'S GUIDELINES

The listener

How well did the listener listen? Any interruptions? Any assumptions? Any body language to **show** listening?

How well did the listener sort out the facts? What sort of questions were asked? Were the facts agreed between the listener and the complainer?

Did the listener apologise if necessary? Was anyone else blamed?

What was the agreed outcome?

The complainer

How well did the complainer state the facts? Did s/he have all the facts?

What did the complainer want done?

How much negotiation went on?

What was the complainer's attitude?

Was the complainer happy with the agreed outcome?

Was it a WIN/WIN situation?

Dealing with complaints from internal customers

Internal customers who complain might be your juniors, your colleagues or your boss. You are probably more inclined to listen to complaints from your boss and do something about them than you are from your juniors or your colleagues, but good business relationships need you to treat all three as equally important. We are talking about real complaints, not just the odd moan.

The sequence is the same as for dealing with internal customers, except that you cannot pass the complaint on if someone is complaining about your work: you have to do something about it yourself. If someone is complaining about working **conditions**, you might have to pass this up the line, but for now we will assume that you have done something that other people do not like. Perhaps you have made a mistake, or made it difficult for someone else to do their job properly.

We will follow the sequence through and see what difference it makes if a complaint comes from an internal customer.

- *Listen*

It is usually harder to listen well if an internal customer complains, because you know instantly that they are getting at you, and your defences go up. Can you listen to someone complaining to you about you? It takes a lot of practice, and is particularly difficult if the complaint is coming from someone junior to you. For example, if your junior has a genuine complaint about your illegible handwriting, do you dismiss the complaint as unimportant, or are you willing to listen properly and well?

- *Sort out the facts – is the complaint justified?*

If the listening is well done, sorting out the facts with an internal customer is usually not too difficult because you are both on the same company wavelength (or should be) and know what you are trying to achieve.

Using the handwriting as an example again, you both want the letter or the report or the message, or whatever it is, to be easily read and typed or interpreted or passed on with a minimum of delay, so you both have the same aim. The facts probably are that most of what you have written is legible, but that certain words or certain letters give trouble.

- *Apologise if necessary*

This is the most difficult part in many cases, because if you apologise you acknowledge you are wrong. Are you strong enough to do this? Are you able to say 'I'm sorry, it's my fault' without blaming others, or difficult circumstances or whatever?

- *Say what you will do to put the matter right*

This is the easy bit if you have gone through all the other steps. If your handwriting, for example, really is illegibile and you acknowledge that it is, agree to write larger, or smaller, or write certain words in capital letters, or use a dictating machine – whatever is suitable for the situation.

Exercise 3

You can do the same exercise as you did with the external customer, but make it a colleague, a boss or a junior who is complaining this time. Use the handwriting example if you like. If you are the complainer, make sure you have a sample of the writing you are complaining about, so that you can be specific about your facts.

Points to remember from this chapter

Making complaints
- Make sure your complaint is well founded
- Complain to the right person – someone who can do something about it
- Collect your facts
- State the facts clearly and reasonably
- Say what you want done
- Be prepared to negotiate
- Agree the outcome
- Don't be aggressive

Dealing with complaints
- Listen
- Sort out the facts
- Apologise if necessary
- Don't blame others
- Say what is going to happen next
- Don't go on the defensive

8 Working with Other People

In this chapter:
- The basics of good teamwork
  - Know your goals
  - Plan to achieve them
  - Communicate
  - Use people's abilities
  - Recognition and encouragement
- Know yourself
  - Know your strengths
  - Recognise your weaknesses
  - Recognise when things cannot change
  - Recognise when things should not change

The basics of good teamwork

This chapter is about the basics of good teamwork, and how to work with other people to achieve a task. Start by doing a group exercise to see how well you can work with others as a team.

Exercise 1

Do this in fours. Start when someone gives the signal and see which team of four gets the right answer first.

Task: You have to write to someone whose **name, house number** and **street name** are given in code.
Work as a team to decode the message.

88

Name: GREATRAM VANOSIDD (anagrams)

House number:
Number of motorway
which links
London and Oxford   . . . . .
Add 2 fat ladies   + ...
                             = ...

Multiply by the number of
20p pieces in a £   ×   . . . . .
                             = ...

Divide by C   ÷   . . . . .
                             = ...

Take away the maximum
number of players on the
field at one time in a
soccer match   −   . . . . .
                             = ...

Street name:
False hair; and without
the last letter, sounds as
if they went on horseback

The answer is towards the end of the chapter.

How well did you work as a team? In your teams of four answer these questions.

1 *Did you know what you were trying to achieve?*
The answer is probably 'yes', because the task was clearly set out.

2 *Did you plan to achieve the goal?*
Probably not: you probably plunged straight into solving the anagrams all together instead of taking time to think and plan who would do what.

3 *Did you communicate?*
Did you tell the others when you knew something?
Did you ask for help when you needed it?
Did you listen to what the others had to say?

4 *Did you use people's abilities?*
Did somebody know about 2 fat ladies being a bingo number and somebody else know about the motorway number and so on? Did you

find out who knew what and who was best at doing what?

5 *How much did you encourage each other?*
Did you say 'well done' when someone did something right? Did you give the winning team a round of applause?

The test you have just completed was not very complicated or difficult. The task itself was not important. What was important was how well you worked as a team, and what goes into good teamwork. Answering questions 1–5 will have helped you analyse what you did and did not do as good team members. We will go through each of the elements in more detail.

Know your goals

Whatever you are doing at work you need to know exactly what you are trying to achieve. Until you do, it is almost impossible to plan. This is why each chapter in this book starts with 'In this chapter . . .'; you know right at the beginning what the chapter is about and what your learning goals are.

Every organisation for which you work will have long-term goals. Business goals are normally about profits and how to achieve them; they will include quality of product, service to customers, keeping the costs down, and so on. A charity's goals will be different; they might be relief of suffering, education or counselling. A public service body, such as your local government, will have different goals again, such as providing first-class local service and spending local income to the best advantage.

Whatever your work, you will be part of the achievement of those long-term goals, and will have your own tasks to perform within the overall plan. You will probably also have personal goals to achieve, such as promotion, better pay and more interesting work.

The organisation's long-term goals will be set by others – the senior management of the organisation. You can set your own personal goals. The difficulty often lies with the bit in the middle: you are not totally sure of what you are trying to achieve, either because nobody has explained to you, or because they have explained it badly, or because you have not understood. If you do not know what you are supposed to be doing or how you are to do it, ASK. A good team leader will make sure that every member of the team does know what the goals are, but not every leader is good at the job of leading. If your boss or team leader is not very good at explaining what is wanted, keep asking until you are clear.

ASK

Plan to achieve them

Organisations have their corporate plans. You might have your own plans for how to achieve your personal goals. You also need to plan how to achieve the tasks you do at work.

Your boss or team leader should have taken time to think and plan who is going to do what and when it is to be done. You, in your turn, have to plan how you are going to achieve your particular bit of the task.

For example, if you are working in an office and a whole lot of work lands on your desk, you know that you have to take time to sift through it, see what the priorities and deadlines are, and decide in which order you are going to tackle it. Dealing with whatever happens to be on top of the pile will not normally be an efficient way of working. If you are assembling something, or setting out a display, you need to plan how to collect the parts you need and then in what order to put the thing together.

More mistakes are made and more time lost by people plunging straight into detail, particularly if they are pressed for time, than by almost anything else they do or do not do at work.

PLAN

Communicate

As you know, communication is a two-way process and means listening as well as talking. We have already thought about listening in many situations. Listening is also part of being a good member of the team.

What about talking, or writing, as part of a team? It goes without saying that you will do everything you can if someone asks you for help or information. Being a really good person to work with means anticipating what other people need, letting them know about it before they ask. For example, if you were doing the anagrams in Exercise 1, but happened to see that another person in your team would need to know what '2 fat ladies' means, you could **offer** the information rather than letting them struggle. Put yourself in the other person's shoes and think about what they will need so that they can do the job properly.

COMMUNICATE

Use people's abilities

Your team leader, or boss, should use the different abilities of the members of the team to achieve the total task in the best and most efficient way. For example, if the task needs something writing down, the team leader should find out who likes writing and is good at it; we usually enjoy things we are good at. Some people are very experienced at certain things, and will therefore do them well; others may have an artistic flair, which can be used in certain circumstances. Some people have very logical minds, and are good administrators. Some like number crunching and are generally good with figures.

If you are new to a team, the team leader will need to find out what you are good at and enjoy doing. Do not resent being asked what you can do (unless people ask, they will not know); and do not be afraid to volunteer information about what you enjoy doing, or do well. If you volunteer to do something, you are more likely to be given things you enjoy doing.

USE ABILITIES

Recognition and encouragement

This is often the most neglected part of teamwork. People forget to say 'well done' or 'thank you' or to show recognition or appreciation.

We all need recognition for what we do, and work better if we get it. Nobody is asking anybody to go over the top and go around handing out bouquets left, right and centre; a simple 'thank you' is often enough.

Your team leader should remember to thank you or say well done (when you **have** done something well). You need that recognition to go on and do more. You should thank your colleagues for that extra bit of help they gave you, or for saving you from making an embarrassing mistake. You should encourage people by saying 'well done' or 'that was a good job' – or words to that effect, if you really mean it. You must mean what you say or it will do no good.

People often **think** that others are doing well, but just do not remember to say so; they say when something is wrong, but not when something is right. If everyone on a team tries to be positive sometimes, as well as negative, the team works better together and the total task becomes easier.

Recognition and encouragement do not only have to come down the line – they can go up the line as well. Bosses are human, too, and need recognition just as much as anyone else. If you think your boss has been particularly helpful, or has done something really well, say so. It might seem an unusual thing to do, and your boss might be a bit surprised, but it will do wonders for your working relationships.

RECOGNISE

Exercise 2

Now do the second team task, but this time actively try to do the following:

1 Agree exactly what you are trying   ASK
   to achieve
2 Plan how you are going to work   PLAN
3 Listen and anticipate the needs of   COMMUNICATE
   others
4 Find out who can do what and   USE ABILITIES
   who likes doing what
5 Recognise when the others do   RECOGNISE
   things well and say so

     Work in the same fours as before to do this task:

Find out the name and full address and telephone number of this person:

Name: SHENPET MANTHIOL

House number:

   Number of motorway which
   links Manchester and Leeds   .....
   Multiply by the number of
   inches in a foot   ×   .....
     = ...

   Divide by the number of
   players in a doubles
   tennis match   ÷   .....
     = ...

   Take away the highest
   possible 3-dart score   −   .....
     = ...

   Add a baker's dozen   + ...
     = ...

Street name:

   The largest island in
   the Caribbean + a shape
   of the moon

Town:

   Inside 'the prison and over the top'

Postcode:
Fill in the missing words or letters
- SO.....
- One of two ..... in a pod
- 2020 is twenty past .....
- One, ..., buckle my shoe
- .....KL
- They have their ..... its and their entrances

Telephone number:
Zero + 2(= ?) × 3 − 2
Trio − 1 × 2 + 3 − 5 + 4

When you have finished the task, analyse how well you worked as a team. Did you:
- KNOW THE GOALS?
- PLAN?
- COMMUNICATE?
- USE ABILITIES?
- ENCOURAGE AND RECOGNISE?

Incidentally, the solution to Exercise 1 is: Margaret Davidson 42 Wigan Road.
You will find the solution to Exercise 2 at the end of the chapter.

Know yourself

Know your strengths; recognise your weaknesses

How good are you at working with other people? Answer the following quiz by ticking a, b, c or d for each statement.
    a = almost always
    b = most of the time
    c = not often
    d = almost never
For example, for the statement 'I enjoy the work I do', this would be:
    a = 'I almost always enjoy the work I do'
    b = 'Most of the time I enjoy the work I do'
    c = 'I do not often enjoy the work I do'
    d = 'I almost never enjoy the work I do'

94

Other people quiz

Here are the statements about **working with other people**. It is important to be honest about this. Tick a, b, c or d.

	a	b	c	d
1 If I don't know what I'm doing, I ask someone				
2 When I'm not busy, I ask if there is anything to do				
3 I check that the details are right				
4 I get bored easily				
5 I say when something is wrong				
6 I listen to what I'm told				
7 I forget to say 'thank you'				
8 I plunge straight into detail				
9 I read instructions carefully				
10 I actually tell people when they've done something well				
11 I shout at people				
12 I anticipate what others need				

a = almost always
b = most of the time
c = not often
d = almost never

How honest were you and how well did you do? Check your ticks against the grid on page 97: for example, if you put a tick in 'a' for Question 1, score 4; if your tick is in 'b', score 3 and so on.

How many did you get out of 48? Anything above 40, you are probably good at working with other people; well done. Between 30 and 40, pretty good. Between 20 and 30, you need to work at it. If you got under 20 it sounds as though you are not very happy working where you are and with the people around you: is there something you can do about it? There usually is.

Whatever your score was, read these comments and then make a plan to improve your own business relationships.

Q1 Always ask if you do not know. It is a strength to ask for help, not a weakness.
Q2 Offer help, rather than waiting to be asked.
Q3 If you get details wrong, it could have disastrous effects somewhere else in the team (see Chapter 11).
Q4 OK. Try to find something more interesting to do. Learn some more about your work, so that you can be given something better to do.
Q5 You should say when something is wrong, but say it to the right person and in the right way (see Chapter 7).
Q6 Do listen. It helps you and the others.
Q7 A lot of people do; you might have to make a special effort.
Q8 Stop and think – it will save you time in the end.
Q9 Do not assume or skim: read instructions slowly, and aloud if necessary.
Q10 If you do, good for you. Some people find it very difficult to do this.
Q11 It does no good.
Q12 Thinking ahead is a good way of planning and helping others in the team.

Practice

If you have been honest in your self-assessment about how well you work with other people and want to improve your business relationships, make yourself a plan.

1 Fill in the following list.

MY STRENGTHS (What I do well)	MY WEAKNESSES (What I could do better or more often)
1.	1.
2.	2.
3.	3.

Under each heading list three things that you know about yourself. You can use the Other people quiz and comments on pages 94 and 95 as your guide.

2 Choose two of your weaknesses.

3. For each weakness write down:
    (a) what you are going to do to improve
    (b) when you are going to do it.
    Be as specific as you can. For example, if you have written down one of your weaknesses as 'I don't ask for help often enough', you could plan:
    (a) 'I don't understand or I can't do (something definite) and I will ask (write down a person's name) for help.
    (b) (Write a definite day and time – eg tomorrow morning, or Wednesday next week or whatever).

4 Put the plan into action.

Question no	a	b	c	d
1	4	3	2	1
2	4	3	2	1
3	4	3	2	1
4	1	2	3	4
5	4	3	2	1
6	4	3	2	1
7	1	2	3	4
8	1	2	3	4
9	4	3	2	1
10	4	3	2	1
11	1	2	3	4
12	4	3	2	1

Recognise when things cannot change

One essential of working with other people is to be able to recognise when things cannot change, at least for a while, and learning to work with things as they are.

Here are some examples of situations which cannot change; in each case say what you would do to make working life in these situations reasonable, without changing jobs:

1 **The transport**. Your public transport to work is unreliable; sometimes you arrive very early and sometimes late. You know there is nothing you can do about the public transport. Write down your ideas for living with this problem.

2 **The boss**. You and the others find your boss very difficult to work for: s/he is unfair, lazy and unapproachable, but is all smiles when management comes around. You can see no possibility of your boss being moved. How can you continue to work with him or her?

3 **The equipment**. The machinery or equipment you have to use is out-of-date and keeps breaking down. The company is short of money and has stated flatly that there are no funds for investing in new equipment and machinery for at least six months, and probably longer. How can you carry on with your work?

4 **The layout**. The layout of your place of work means that you spend a lot of time going from place to place to deliver things or fetch things. For example, perhaps the photocopier you have to use is on another floor. You cannot alter the layout of the building, nor can you get the photocopier moved. What can you do to save yourself some time and aggravation?

What were your solutions to these annoying situations? In the end you might just have to get your head down and get on with the job as it is, but there are things in each situation which you could do to make life more bearable. Grumbling will not help. Grumbling makes no difference to the situation and makes you and others feel negative; working with people who are negative all the time is no joke. So what could you do?

Situation 1 – **The transport**
(a) Find someone else in the company who lives in roughly the same direction and ask to share their private transport. Offer to pay a reasonable amount and be prepared to go out of your way a little to get to the pickup point – the extra exercise will do you good!

(b) Negotiate with your boss so that your early arrival compensates for the times when you are late. Make sure your boss understands your problems. Make sure the others understand your problems, too, and the solution you have worked out with your boss, so that it does not seem as though you are getting preferential treatment.

(c) Work through breaks or go home later on the days when you are late, if that is feasible.

(d) Leave home earlier, so that you are always early, but leave promptly at the end of the day.

The real message here is that you cannot change the public transport system, but you can try ways round it. Above all, ask other people to help you sort out the problem: if they do not know about it they cannot understand and cannot help. It depends on the job you do and how flexible your timekeeping can be.

Situation 2 – **The boss**

It is very tempting, in this situation, to gang up on the boss and make life as unpleasant for him or her as s/he is making it for you. If this happens, behaviour breeds behaviour and a totally negative situation grows up. You cannot get yourself or the boss moved, so what can you do?

(a) Don't join in any anti-boss 'gang'.

(b) Ask yourself why your boss is like that; try to understand what makes him/her tick.

(c) Try to get on the same wavelength as your boss, perhaps by talking about things which interest him/her in work or outside it. If s/he does something well or good, recognise it and say so, without being sarcastic and 'smarmy'. Getting a reputation as 'teacher's pet' will not help you.

(d) If you really cannot get on, do your work as well as you can and keep out of the way.

(e) Use the situation as a learning experience of what not to do when you become the boss.

In this situation do all you can to get on with the boss, rather than antagonising him or her. Keeping a low profile and learning from the experience might be the only solution in the end.

Situation 3 – **The equipment**

You know you have got to use this equipment for some time to come. Here are some ideas about what to do:

(a) Treat the equipment properly, so it breaks down as seldom as possible.

(b) Make friends with the engineer, or whoever has to mend it when it breaks down. If the engineer does not mind coming to you, because you are easy to work with, s/he is more likely to come when wanted and to do what can be done with the equipment.

(c) Think of alternative ways of producing whatever it is you want to do, so that you have some sort of backup system available, even if it means doing something by hand.

(d) Have your case well prepared, so that when the time comes when money can be spent, you can get in first with a well-presented request for new equipment (see Chapter 7).

Situation 4 – **The layout**
If you are stuck with doing a lot of running around, think about doing something like this:

(a) Do the work in batches, so that you can collect or deliver (or use the photocopier for) several jobs at once.

(b) Think about the route you have to take and plan to do other things on the way there or on the way back, so that you do not have to make double journeys.

(c) Arrange with a friend who has to do similar trips that you will share the running around and do some for each other.

(d) See if there is anyone who will make the **opposite** journey, so that they can bring things to you and you take things to them while you are doing your own work.

(e) Be positive about how much exercise you are getting, and that you have a break from your desk or work station every now and then!

There are things at work which cannot be changed, but there is often something which can be done to change other things around the unchangeable. Do not be bound by barriers which seem to be unsurmountable. Very often they are not as fixed as you think. Think creatively (see Chapter 12).

Recognise when things should not change

Rules
There are occasions when things should not change, however unreasonable they may seem to you. In these situations you must stick to the rules. You are not a wimp if you obey these rules – you are stupid if you do not. Here are some examples:

1 **Safety:** your employers have an obligation under the Health and Safety at Work Act 1974 to make your working life as healthy and safe as they possibly can. You, too, have an obligation under the Act to follow the safety rules and not do anything which would endanger yourself or anyone else.

2 **Security:** there are always rules about security in any business. They could be about how money should be handled, wearing or carrying security passes, locking drawers and doors, looking after personal property etc.

3 **Law:** your employer will have certain legal obligations in addition to the Health and Safety at Work Act. There are laws about employment contracts, the Data Protection Act, the Trades Description Act etc which must be obeyed. Do not try to cut corners on these things – know the rules (find out about them if necessary) and stick to them.

4 **Emergencies:** your employers will have definite procedures in the case of an emergency (a fire, or a bomb threat). These procedures are worked out with the help of the police and the fire brigade and must be followed. There are also fire precautions which must be taken. For example, if there is a notice on a door saying 'Fire Door, Keep Shut', keep it shut, and do not wedge it open with a fire extinguisher, however hot the weather.

The examples you have just read are all about rules and regulations which must be obeyed. In any organisation there are usually unwritten rules or conventions which have come to be accepted by all concerned because they benefit the majority of the people who work there. Others will find you easy to work with if you follow these conventions too. Here are some examples:

Conventions or 'house rules'
1 House style for the layout of documents (letters, reports etc). They reflect the company image and make it easier for support staff (WP operators etc).

2 Deadlines for information: for example, ringing in to say you are sick, or booking your holiday dates, or getting data to another department.

3 Personal telephone calls, in and out. If you abuse these privileges the conventions might be tightened for everyone.

4 Cover at break or holiday times. If you are asked to change your own arrangements so that cover can be provided, do what you can to help.

5 Dress. This can be a really burning topic – people spend hours talking about it at staff meetings. Once the convention has been agreed, follow it.

6 People's territory (see Chapter 3). In some organisations there are certain 'no go' areas for junior staff; sometimes people have places where they always sit in meetings or in the staff restaurant. Be sensitive about these conventions, and observe them where you can.

7 Smoking: some companies have definite house rules about where you may or may not smoke. If those rules exist, obey them. If there are no definite rules, be sensitive about working with non-smokers.

All these rules, regulations and conventions have been thought up or written down or have just grown to make working life as safe and comfortable for everyone as possible. They help everyone to work with others, as part of the total company or organisation team; obey the definite rules and follow the conventions where they are in the best interests of the majority.

Points to remember from this chapter

- Know what you are trying to achieve
- If you don't know, ask
- Plan how to do something – don't plunge into detail
- Communicate
- Listen and anticipate the needs of others
- Make use of people's differing abilities
- Encourage and recognise achievement
- Bosses are human too
- Know your strengths
- Plan to improve on your weak points
- Find ways of dealing with things which cannot change
- Stick to the rules
- Follow the reasonable conventions

The solution to Exercise 2 is Stephen Hamilton, 19 Cuba Crescent, Andover SP8 2JX. Telephone 0264 324726.

9 Working through Other People

In this chapter:
- Making requests
- Giving instructions
- Motivating
- Delegating
- On the receiving end

Making requests

At work you will be asking other people to do things. You might be the boss, even if you have only one member of staff, or you might have to work through people in another part of the company.

For example, if you are a member of the support staff in one department (working in accounts or wages or with word processors, or are a personal assistant or personal secretary) a lot of your work will be done through people in your own department and in other departments. You might have to collect information from many different sources; you might have to arrange a meeting for several senior members of staff; you might have to contact people with queries. In all these cases you will be carrying out your work through other people.

Of course, if you are the boss in charge of a number of people you will be the leader of that particular team, and you will be working through those people as well as through people in other parts of the company. You will be asking people to do things for you.

There is a difference between ordering people to do things and asking them to do things in such a way that they **want** to do things for you. If you are in a uniformed service, like the police, the fire service or the armed forces, you expect to give and take orders. However, in the general business world if you order people to do something they will probably do it, but will only make a minimum effort. If you can motivate people into wanting to do things, they are much more likely to do them well.

There are times when it is necessary to order someone to do something. When safety is in question you would sometimes have to say 'Do it, and do it now'; you would back this up with a firm tone of voice and the appropriate body language – authoritative and in charge. Sometimes, too, when you have tried every other way of persuading someone to do something properly and they still do it badly, the only thing left to do is to say 'Do it this way, because I say so and it's the way I want it done'. This ought to be a last resort, because it means you have not convinced the person that they should do something in a certain way to your standards. You cannot win with everyone all the time, and sometimes you do have to resort to these tactics. However, the better way to work through people is to ask them to do something, not order them to do it.

You might be making a request of almost anybody – people who are junior to you, people on your level in your team, people on your level in other parts of the company or people who are senior to you but do things for you. For example, you might be a secretary who has to go through the word processing supervisor or the post room supervisor to get things done for you and therefore for your boss. Get this type of business relationship wrong, and you could really have a hard time.

Here is a 4-point plan for asking someone to do something for you. It applies at any level.

1 Know what you want
2 Go through the right channels
3 Ask for what you want directly, clearly and politely
4 When it is done, say thank you

Use this plan to do the following two exercises on your own or with your neighbour.

Exercise 1: *The receptionist*

Imagine you are a receptionist in a firm of about 20 people. You have been asked to make a list of all staff, including Directors, who will be working in the building on the morning of Christmas Eve. The building will close for Christmas at 1.00 pm. The people who run the building want to know from a security point of view exactly who will be there. You have decided to gather this information by 'phone in your quiet moments. How would you go about collecting this information? What would you say on the 'phone?

Exercise 2: *Overtime*

You are in charge of a small team of six people, and need one of them to work overtime on a Friday night to help you with a special project. They normally all go home at 5.30 sharp, especially on a Friday. How would you get one of them to do this extra work?

When you have decided what to do in each case, check your thoughts with these ideas.

1 Know what you want
   ● **The receptionist**
   This is not difficult, all you need to know is who will be in the building **at any time** during the morning of Christmas Eve.
   ● **Overtime**
   You want one person to work overtime on Friday evening, but you need to be clear how long the job is likely to take. Will you need a man or a woman? Will it matter?

2 Go through the right channels
   The receptionist
   ● You can 'phone some people direct, but for others you might have to go through secretaries or assistants or supervisors.
   ● Don't waste people's time when you could get the information from someone else, but don't tread on people's toes by missing them out.
   Overtime
   ● Will you get all the team together, put the question to them and ask for a volunteer, or will you ask one person you think might be willing to do this?
   ● Have you taken into account those you **know** have to get home promptly, and those who could do with the extra money?
   ● Do you always ask favours of the same people, or always give the same people the perks?

3 Ask for what you want directly, clearly and politely
The receptionist
- Tell people **why** you want this information.
- Make it clear that you need to know for any time up until 1.00 pm.
- If people don't know, give them a deadline for getting the information to you.

Overtime
- Say what the project is and what the work will be.
- Say what time you are likely to finish.
- Explain what provision there is for extra coffee/tea.
- Say they will be working with you.
- **Ask** if they are willing, or who is willing to do the overtime.

4 Say thank you
The receptionist
- Say thank you at the end of each 'phone conversation.
- If people have made a special effort to get back to you with the information, thank them on the 'phone and again later when you see them in Reception.

Overtime
- Thank anyone who volunteers.
- Thank the person who does the work – perhaps with a drink?

These are straightforward situations, but there were mistakes to be made. For example, in Reception, if you do not say why you want the information, or you go through the wrong channels, you could put people's backs up. In Overtime if you just tell somebody to stay and do overtime, you might get the wrong person; if you do not tell people exactly what the job is and how long it is likely to last, you could give a false impression. For example, if you said 'Oh, it'll only take an hour' when you know it will take at least two, the person doing the job will probably get very fidgety after an hour and be unable to concentrate properly.

Be clear in your own mind about what you want, and ask for it in a direct way.

 ## Giving instructions

Giving instructions needs clear thinking, too. Giving instructions is not quite the same as making a request, and is different from giving orders. Giving instructions is telling people, usually your juniors, what you want and how you want it done. It is not training, or teaching them (which is often called 'giving instruction' without the 's'), because they know how to do things; they want to know, and need to know, exactly what you want done and how you want it done.

The difference between giving instruction (when people learn how to do things) and giving instructions (when people need to know how you want things done) seems small but is distinct. For example, you might give someone instruction in how to use the photocopier (they learn how to use the machine); later you might give them instructions about how you want something photocopied (two sets on green paper, please). Chapter 8 in *Self Presentation Skills* is about showing someone how to do something. Giving instructions is about setting standards and getting someone else to produce exactly what is wanted.

This time there is a 6-point plan to follow:

1 Know exactly what you want done
2 Choose the right person for the job
3 Give instructions clearly, remembering to say why it is to be done and when it is needed
4 Check that the person has understood you
5 Leave the person to get on with it
6 Give recognition for a job well done.

We will take an example of a boss giving instructions to a junior to ring a colleague called Mrs Bowman to alter a meeting time and fax some papers through.

1 **Know exactly what you want done**
Things can go wrong if you
• are vague about the revised time
• have not sorted out which papers need to be faxed

2 **Choose the right person for the job**
• You might not have a choice, but if you have, choose someone who is good on the 'phone and can work the fax

3 **Give instructions clearly**
Say
• who needs to be contacted
• the revised time of the meeting: give a definite time – 'later in the afternoon' is too vague
• why you need to change the time
• which papers are to be faxed: be precise – 'the report on my desk' could be ambiguous
• to whom the papers are to be faxed: do not assume your junior

knows to whom the papers are to go. It could be to Mrs Bowman or someone quite different
- exactly when the papers are needed: again, be precise – are they needed two days, two hours or two minutes before the meeting, for example

4 Check understanding

If this a routine sort of job and you know your junior well, a glance to read the body language is probably enough to tell you whether all your instructions have been clear. When you have to give instructions, watch the other person's reactions.

If you give these sorts of instructions to someone new to the job, check that the junior knows how to carry them all out. Do not assume that the junior knows where to find 'phone and fax numbers, nor even who Mrs Bowman is. A useful thing to do is to ask the junior to repeat the instructions back to you. This will soon reveal any gaps in knowledge.

5 Leave the person to get on with it

If you have done everything right so far, you can with confidence leave your junior to make the 'phone call and fax the papers without fussing around. You can be getting on with something else.

If your junior is new, encourage him or her to come to you if there are any problems. New people need to know there is someone to turn to if they need help.

6 Give recognition for a job well done

If the job is routine and straightforward for your junior, you do not need to give special recognition for every job. You could say thank you every now and again: 'It's been a good day – thank you'. You could say thank you for something done exceptionally promptly or well: 'Thanks for faxing those papers through so quickly. It was a great help'.

If your junior is new, make a special effort to give encouragement and recognition. It will help build his or her confidence.

The mistake most often made in giving instructions is that people are not clear exactly what they want done, or they do not tell others exactly how to do it. They assume that people are mind-readers, and leave out all sorts of vital details. If you think logically and are clear in your own mind you stand a better chance of conveying this to others.

109

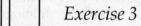 *Exercise 3*

You are to give someone in your group instructions on how to get
from your place of work to somewhere of your choice about a five
minute walk away. Use the 6-point plan to give them your
instructions and see whether they get to the right place. They should
not be gone more than ten minutes!

Here are some guidelines to help you with Exercise 3:

1 **Know what you want done**
   Have you chosen somehere precise and easily recognisable?
2 **Choose the right person**
   Will you choose someone who knows the area and might not follow
   your instructions, or someone who does not know the area?
3 **Give instructions clearly**
   Take time to get your instructions right
4 **Check understanding**
   How will you check that the person knows where s/he is going?
5 **Let them get on with it**
   You can only trust them and wait for them to come back!
6 **Recognise a job well done**
   Don't forget the 'well done' if they get it right; give yourself a pat on
   the back, too. They would not have got there without clear
   instructions

Motivating

If you want to work through others you need to make them want to
work for you. You need to motivate them. Different people are
motivated by different things. Some go to work only for the money; they
do their day's work adequately, keep to time and take no interest in the
business or the company beyond their immediate working
environment. These people are difficult to motivate to become good
members of a team, although the work they do is valuable. Fortunately
there are very few people who go to work solely for the money.

Most people want job satisfaction. They need to know and feel that
they are doing something worthwhile and to see some results at the end
of the day. These people are normally easy to motivate if they are treated
well and given a variety of work to do.

Some people are definitely interested in promotion and taking more responsibility. These people are normally self-motivated. They are the ones who will be asking questions, offering to do other jobs and finding out about the business. They could well be taking courses at college or by distance learning and will want to pick your brains and learn all they can from you.

Almost everyone wants to feel secure in their work, particularly in times of recession. You will not be able to do anything about the overall profitability of the business, but you can make sure that members of your staff feel secure in the work they do by keeping them informed about changes that will affect them in their day-to-day tasks.

A few people work quite happily for very little pay at a boring job for the companionship of being out of the home and with other people. This does not mean that they chat all the time, but they would not be happy working on their own.

As a supervisor or manager you need to be able to decide what motivates each member of your team, and act accordingly. For example, do not try to push someone further than they want to go, although there is no harm in encouraging people to do more than they think they can sometimes.

Exercise 4

Whatever people's motives are for going to work, they will nearly all want to be treated like human beings doing worthwhile work in a secure environment. Here are some ways you, as a boss, can meet these needs.

1 Draw the following chart for yourself.

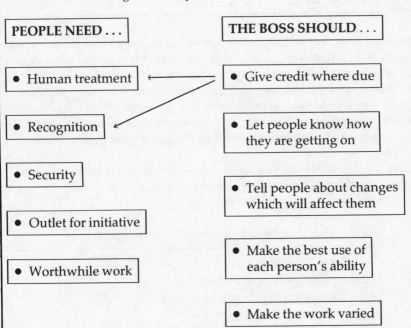

| PEOPLE NEED ... | THE BOSS SHOULD ... |

- Human treatment
- Recognition
- Security
- Outlet for initiative
- Worthwhile work

- Give credit where due
- Let people know how they are getting on
- Tell people about changes which will affect them
- Make the best use of each person's ability
- Make the work varied

2 Take each right-hand box and draw an arrow connecting it to an appropriate left-hand box or boxes. The chart shows how '**Give credit where due**' connects with '**Human treatment**' and '**Recognition**'. If you think it connects with any of the other boxes, draw an arrow to those boxes as well. When you have finished with '**Give credit where due**' go on to '**Let people know how they are getting on**'.

When you have completed your chart you will see how these ways of motivating people (the right-hand boxes) match the needs of your staff (the left-hand boxes). Your chart will probably look like a confused spider's web!

There is one great motivator which we have not mentioned so far. **You** are, or should be, a great motivator in how you do your own work. You are a role model for your staff. Behaviour breeds behaviour. If you are positive, enthusiastic and hard working, your staff are likely to follow your example. If you are a grumbler, are slipshod and lazy, they will almost certainly work in the same way.

 # Delegating

One very good way of keeping people motivated is to give them added responsibility. It also helps you with your time management and means that you do not have to do everything and you are developing others.

Many people, when they delegate, just say to someone 'look after that for me, would you', leave them to it and then wonder why things are not done as they should be. You can sometimes throw people in at the deep end to test their initiative, but it is not a good idea to test it all the time.

When you delegate, you are giving someone full responsibility for doing something. This is where delegation differs from giving instructions. Follow this 6-point plan:

1 Decide what you should and should not delegate
2 Decide to whom you should delegate
3 Give that person all the information and/or training necessary
4 Tell the person where to go for help
5 Leave the person to get on with the job
6 Give credit when the job is well done

You will see that this is very like the 6-point plan for giving instructions, with two important exceptions. One is what you can delegate and what you should do yourself, and the other is that you might need to give the person some training as well as information. It is very unfair, and unproductive, to delegate a job to someone without giving them the proper training to do the job.

It takes time to show someone how to do things, and they are bound to be slower than you are to start with. This is one of the reasons why people do not delegate enough: it is quicker to do it yourself. In the end you will save time if you delegate, but you have to invest a little time in the first place.

When you are deciding **what** you should delegate, try to sort out what only you, as a supervisor or manager, should do and what you can sensibly ask others to do. For example, there may be company rules

which say that only managers or supervisors can hold certain keys, for
security reasons; in such a case you would not delegate to a junior tasks
needing those keys. When you are away, another supervisor or manager
would have to take over those responsibilities. Do not delegate any tasks
which **only** a supervisor or manager should do.

 ## On the receiving end

You will, at sometime during your working life, be on the receiving end
of all these activities. People will be working through you and they will:
- ask you to do things for them
- give you instructions about what they want
- try to motivate you
- delegate tasks to you

Good supervisors or managers, who do all these things well, will make
your work much more interesting and satisfying, but they will need
your cooperation and willingness. Working through other people has to
be a two-way, not a one-way, process.

At the same time as you are doing what you are asked, or taking on
new responsibilities, try to stand back and see how well your manager
or supervisor handles the situation. You can do the good things yourself
when you come to be in that position, and make up your mind not to do
the things which were not so well done. You can learn a lot about
building business relationships with those who are junior to you by
watching and learning from how your boss builds business
relationships with you.

Practice

1 Consider your own working situation and decide on a task in which you can practise:
   - making a request or
   - giving instructions or
   - delegating

   Choose something which you do in the normal course of your work or study.

2 Consciously plan how you are going to tackle whatever you have decided to do, using the appropriate 4- or 6-point plan from this chapter.

3 Carry out whatever you have decided to do, then analyse how well you did it, and decide what you could do better next time. Did you, for example, give precise and clear instructions, or did you leave out some detail? Did you check that the other person understood what you were asking him or her to do? Did you give credit where it was due, or remember to say thank you?

Once you have done this sort of thing well in a small way, you will find it much easier to tackle something bigger next time, and you will be on the way to managing or supervising people successfully.

Points to remember from this chapter

- Ask, don't order
- Decide what you want to do
- Go through the right people
- Be clear in your instructions
- Check understanding
- Leave people to get on with things
- Let people know how they are getting on
- Tell people about changes which will affect them
- Use people's abilities
- Give credit where due

10 Self Development Opportunities

In this chapter:
How to get the best out of
- Appraisals
- Assessments
- Self-study
- Training courses
- Work experience

In your working life, or in your school or college life, there will be many different opportunities for you to develop your knowledge and skills and to learn new techniques. When these opportunities arise, make the most of them.

 ## Appraisals

Most medium-sized and big companies and many small companies run an appraisal system. This system normally allows you to sit down with your immediate manager and talk about how you have performed over a certain period of time and to discuss your strengths and weaknesses. This is usually done by your manager filling in an appraisal form about your work performance and then arranging an appraisal interview with you. Most appraisals are done once a year. A good appraisal system will encourage you to plan, with your line manager, what you need to learn to develop your knowledge and skills further, and how to get the necessary training.

Some appraisal systems are not so helpful, and merely tell you what you did well and where you could improve, without giving you a chance to discuss what further training you need. This is more of a report than a proper appraisal. In some systems the person one up from your immediate line manager will do the appraisal with you; this is not usually as satisfactory as your line manager doing the appraisal, because your line manager is the person who knows your work best. A system often allows your line manager's boss to add comments to the appraisal form, which you may or may not be allowed to see.

The most helpful appraisals from your point of view are those which are totally open, so that you know what people think of your work, what your prospects are and what you have to do to develop your skills and knowledge. For example, if you know that your boss thinks you could get promotion if you prove that you are good at your present job for another six months, and take a particular training course or course of self-study, you know exactly where you stand and how to get that promotion.

Some appraisal systems are linked into the pay structure, and you get rewarded for good work by extra pay. Most good appraisal systems are used to let management know whether you are ready for promotion or not.

Some systems encourage you to prepare for your appraisal interview by asking you to think about and write down your thoughts on your progress over the last year, and to set yourself targets for the coming year. If you are working with this sort of system, use the preparation time and the form provided and do your own preparation as thoroughly as possible.

In many systems you will be asked to sign to say that you agree with what has been put on the appraisal form; there is usually an opportunity for you to write down anything with which you do not agree. Take this part of the system seriously, and if you genuinely think that someone has written something wrong about your work, say so. Word your remarks carefully to show that you have thought about what you are going to write and are not being emotional about it.

Sometimes appraisals do not go well, which can be very frustrating because you feel you have wasted your one opportunity in the year to talk about you, your work performance and your plans. There could be several reasons for an unproductive appraisal; they could be:

1 You have not prepared properly
2 You cannot admit to certain weaknesses
2 You have not been given time to prepare properly
4 The appraisal interview is rushed or interrupted
5 Your boss does not give you enough chance to say what you want to do
6 Your boss has written remarks with which you totally disagree
7 The two of you don't get on

Here are a few comments under each of those headings:

1 **You have not prepared properly**
If you realise that the appraisal interview is going badly because you have not done enough preparation, apologise and ask if you can stop the interview and arrange another date.

2 **You cannot admit to certain weaknesses**
If you find it difficult to agree that you do something badly, ask for specific examples. Then you must be really honest with yourself, and either agree that you could improve or disagree and write your disagreement on the form.

3 **You have not been given time to prepare properly**
You are normally given at least a couple of days to prepare for an appraisal interview. If you think the notice you are given is too short, say so and arrange another appointment.

4 **The appraisal interview is rushed or interrupted**
If you feel that the interview has not been properly completed, do not sign the form and ask to arrange another time to meet. This is not very satisfactory, but it is better than waiting a whole year.

5 **Your boss does not give you enough chance to say what you want to do**
If your boss is not a good manager and will not listen to what you have to say, it is very difficult to do anything at the time of the interview. This depends on your character and how confident you are that you can make people listen to you; it also depends on how good your preparation was. If you come out of this interview and know that you have not got your point across because you did not have the courage, try writing down what you wanted to say, tell your boss as soon as you can that there were one or two other things you wanted to mention and hand over what you have written down.

6 **Your boss has written remarks with which you totally disagree**
The only thing you can do here is say that you disagree with what is written and either refuse to sign the form or add to the form that you disagree and then sign it. After the appraisal interview you might want to take the matter further. Many companies have an official appeals procedure; if there is one in your company, use it. It may be that your union representative can help you. Otherwise go to your manager's boss and explain what has happened. Remember that your appraisal will sit in your personnel file for the rest of your working life with that company, so the information on that file should be correct.

7 **The two of you don't get on**

It is important to keep emotion out of appraisals; if you are both determined that your appraisal will be done in a formal, professional way, and you both look at each part of the form objectively, it is possible to have a fair appraisal even when you do not like each other. If you know that this will not work, you can ask for your appraisal to be done by someone else, although that person is not likely to know your work quite so well. If you have had the appraisal and it has gone badly you will probably need to go to your manager's boss for help. This does not happen very often – most managers try to be fair over appraisals.

Whenever it is time for your appraisal, use this checklist.

Appraisal checklist
- Prepare properly
- Assess your own strengths and weaknesses objectively
- Know how you want to progress
- Listen to what your manager has to say
- Put your own point of view
- Plan your progress for the next year, setting targets where possible
- Complete the paperwork
- Thank your boss for a helpful appraisal, if possible

Assessments

Appraisals are sometimes called assessments, because someone is assessing your work. Assessments in this chapter means judging a task or tasks against a set of targets or criteria. It is the sort of assessment that you have to go through for many certificates: there are certain things which you have to achieve, and when you have done the work someone will assess whether you have achieved what you set out to do, or not.

At school and college you probably have a great deal of your work assessed, and your achievements go towards the examination or certificate you are trying to gain. At work your ability to perform certain tasks to a certain standard is likely to be assessed from time to time. This could be in the normal course of learning the job, or it could be that you are taking further certificates or examinations at work and your supervisor or manager has to assess how competent you are before you can be awarded the certificate. Assessment at work is likely to be on the tasks you do as the normal part of your job.

If you want to think about Oral Assessment, read Chapter 3 of *Self Presentation Skills*.

There are four main stages in the assessment of your competence to do a job:

1 Know what you are aiming at
2 Do the work
3 Prove you can do it
4 Get your assessor to agree you can do it

1 Know what you are aiming at

You will be assessed on your competence in doing a task or a job. For example, the task, which is often called a Unit, might be 'Handling Money'. Within that task there are certain things which you must be able to do to a given standard; the things you have to do within the task (for example, 'carry out cash receipt and payment procedures') are called Elements, and the standards you must reach (eg 'correct change is given') are called Performance Criteria.

Under NVQ (National Vocational Qualifications), the Unit, Elements and Performance Criteria would be set out something like this:

EXAMPLE

UNIT 4: Handling Money

Element 4.1 Carry out cash receipt and payment procedures

Performance Criteria
4.1.1 Laid down procedures for handling cash are correctly followed
4.1.2 Correct change is given
4.1.3 Transactions are recorded accurately and legibly
4.1.4 Laid down security procedures for cash handling are followed

There would be other Elements (for example, Element 4.2 'Handle credit card and cheque transactions') to make up the Unit. You would be assessed on each Element and would have to achieve all the Elements before you can be assessed as competent in the whole Unit.

It is important to know exactly what you are aiming at, so you must look at all the Elements within the Unit, and most of all at the Performance Criteria within the Element. Taking our example of 'Unit 4 – Handling Money', you know you must prove yourself competent in Element 4.1 (Carry out cash receipt and payment procedures), in Element 4.2 (Handle credit card and cheque transactions) and in any other Elements you find in that Unit. It is possible to be given credit for separate Elements, when you do not achieve all the Elements in a Unit.

For each Element (Element 4.1 for example) you have to achieve

all the performance Criteria (4.1.1, 4.1.2, 4.1.3 and 4.1.4). In our example you have to prove that you can: follow the procedures, give the correct change, record the transactions properly and follow the security procedures.

So, there are two things you have to do to know what you are aiming to achieve:

(a) Make sure you have a copy of the Unit, Elements and Performance Criteria

(b) Make sure you understand them.

It is not usually difficult to get a copy of the Unit, Elements and Performance Criteria, but you cannot work without this information, so make sure you get it.

It is often more difficult to understand what the words actually mean. For example, what does 'Transactions are recorded accurately and legibly' mean? It depends where you work and what sort of cash handling you do.

If you work in a shop, you would probably carry out the cash procedures through the till. 'Transactions' would mean ringing up customers' orders on the till, 'accurately' would mean without making mistakes, and being able to correct any mistakes you make, and 'legibly' would mean that the customer can read the till slip because there is enough ink in the machine.

If you work somewhere where a bill is handwritten – a dry cleaners, for example – 'legibly' would mean that your handwriting must be clear.

Before you start a task, or start to learn a task, make sure you **understand what you have to do**, and ask until you do.

2 **Do the work**

This is obvious, but not as simple as it sounds. You must refer to the Performance Criteria to see exactly what you have to do and to what standard. For example, another Element in the 'Handling Money' Unit could be 'Carry out everyday financial transactions'. This Unit is about banking procedures and all sorts of financial systems: one of the Performance Criteria in this Element might be '100% accuracy is achieved regarding figures and amounts'. When doing the work to achieve this Element you know that only 100% accuracy will be accepted. If you were typing or word processing internal memos in another Unit, you might find that 95% accuracy is acceptable.

In some cases you have to carry out a task, or certain Elements within the task, several times before you have achieved the Performance Criteria, because your consistency is being measured.

As you do the work keep an eye on the Performance Criteria, and make sure you have achieved the necessary standards before you go on to the next stage.

3 **Prove you can do it**
There are all sorts of ways to prove that you can do something.
Writing about it is not necessarily the best way, although sometimes it might be.
Here are a few examples of ways in which you can prove that you can do something:

- Accurate cash handling: till slips and reports generated by the cash register
- Creating a database: printout of the database information, plus your written instructions on how to use the database
- Passing on messages: the written message, whether taken on the 'phone or face-to-face, plus a signature to say the person received the message

---

Exercise 1

Here is a list of tasks; beside each one write your ideas of how you could prove to somebody else that you could do the task. What evidence of competence could you produce?

(a) Set up a display

(b) Mailmerge 20 letters

(c) Answer incoming telephone calls

(d) Address an envelope

(e) Know the provisions of the Health and Safety at Work Act as far as it affects you

(f) Sort and distribute incoming mail

(g) Book a hotel conference room

(h) Deal with customer complaints

If you have used your imagination you will have come up with some interesting ideas. Compare your ideas with these:

Task (a): Set up a display
Evidence of competence: A photograph.

Task (b): Mailmerge 20 letters
Evidence of competence: Photocopies of the standard letter, the details to be merged, the name and address file and one copy of the finished article. It would be wasteful to photocopy 20 letters.

Task (c): Answer incoming telephone calls
Evidence of competence: Your supervisor's signature to say you can do this to the required standard. You might back this up with a checklist of what to do when answering the 'phone. You could get an audio tape of yourself answering the calls.

Task (d): Address an envelope
Evidence of competence: a properly addressed envelope, not a pretend one on a sheet of paper.

Task (e): Knowledge of HASAWA
Evidence of competence: it is very difficult to provide evidence for this. A written or an oral test is probably the only way of proving that you have knowledge, as opposed to skills.

Task (f): Sort and distribute incoming mail
Evidence of competence: photocopy of the page where this process is logged, if such a page is filled in. Otherwise a supervisor's signature.

Task (g): Book a hotel conference room
Evidence of competence: photocopy of letter or fax confirming the booking and showing all details.

Task (h): Deal with customer complaints
Evidence of competence: only a supervisor's signature is real proof of your competence, but you could back it up with a checklist of DOs and DON'Ts.

You can see the variety of 'evidence' that you can collect and that some proof is based on your Assessor's signature that you can perform the task to the required standard – that is, that you have met the Performance Criteria.
It is very important that you collect **all** the evidence you need. In

NVQ, for example, your Assessor is likely to be your tutor or immediate line manager, and the person who finally says whether or not you have met the criteria is a Verifier. A Verifier is someone representing an examining body like the RSA, Pitmans, City & Guilds or BTEC who agrees or disagrees with the Assessor's judgement. A Verifier needs all the evidence that you can provide, and needs to be able to find it quickly. Collect all the evidence together, and make sure it is properly filed and easy to find.

4 **Get your Assessor to agree you can do it**
Your Assessor normally has to sign to say that you have reached the standards of the Performance Criteria. To do this your Assessor must know what the Performance Criteria are and what they mean, just as you have to. Therefore, make sure your Assessor:
- has a copy of the Unit, Elements and Performance Criteria
- understands what they mean
- signs you off for an Element or a Unit when you have proved you can do the task

It is up to you to organise when and how your Assessor judges your competence and signs to say that you have achieved the task. Make sure you have all the paperwork you need and have entered in your Log Book or Assessment Record exactly what you did to achieve the task, ready for your Assessor's signature.

If your Assessor does not think you have met all the Performance Criteria, be prepared to improve your performance and/or do the job again to your Assessor's satisfaction. A signature for work which is not up to standard devalues the whole scheme.

Assessment checklist
- Have a copy of each Element you are attempting
- Make sure you understand what you have to do
- Check what you actually do against the Performance Criteria
- Collect all the evidence you can
- Make sure your Assessor understands what you are doing
- File it so that it can easily be found
- Agree your competence with the Assessor
- Get that Element or Unit 'signed off'

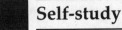

Self-study

Self-study is a growing method of self-development. Its advantages are that you can study at times and places which suit you and above all you can study at your own pace. Its great disadvantage is its lack of motivation through group work or a very close contact with a tutor or trainer; you have to be very disciplined to succeed with self-study.

There are three main branches of self-study:

- Open learning
- Distance learning
- Active learning

They are used for different aspects of learning and each has different characteristics.

● Open Learning

Open learning means that the learning involved is open to all – there are no, or very few, barriers. You do not have to be a particular age, live in a certain place, study at definite times or have specified qualifications. If you lack certain basic knowledge to complete a course of study there is usually a conversion course available.

The Open University, where you study for a degree, and the Open College, where you study things of a more practical nature, are good examples of open learning. The open learning materials are very varied and include books, tapes, videos, computers, radio and television. There are many bodies in addition to the Open University and Open College who offer open learning facilities. Some courses lead to nationally recognised qualifications, others do not. Some have a named tutor to support you and/or residential elements. Some are designed to be supported by your employers, financially and by providing an in-house tutor or trainer. In many open learning packages there is a lot of self-assessment. You prove to yourself that you have mastered one stage before going on to the next. If you are studying for a degree by this method, it is more usual for you to have to write essays which are marked by a tutor, with comments.

Open learning has opened up avenues of learning to all sorts of people who cannot, for example, attend college because they cannot afford the time to study full-time or live too far away to attend a college part-time. It is very much concerned with the development of the individual in a wide range of knowledge, thought and skills.

● Distance learning

Distance learning is allied to open learning and uses many of the open learning techniques, but tends to be organised by employers. They decide whether their employees would benefit from learning certain things, and make learning opportunities available.

From an employer's point of view it is often more cost-effective to provide learning opportunities at a distance rather than asking their employees to attend courses centrally, where they have to pay for travel and accommodation. This is particularly true for large companies with nationwide outlets. Cost-effective does not necessarily mean cheaper; it means better value for money. Employees can learn exactly what they need for self-development in the jobs at their own pace.

For example, a company will often provide supervisory training for newly-promoted employees or people who have reached a certain level within the company. Sometimes this is arranged through the company's training department, which provides the learning material and all necessary support. Often this type of learning is provided by local colleges, with support from their tutors; the learning material can be created by the college or by a nationally recognised body like NEBSS (the National Examinations Board for Supervisory Studies). The work often involves assignments which have to be assessed by a tutor.

Sometimes employers will give people who are learning through this route time to study during working hours. Others might pay for the course and expect employees to study in their own time.

Again the learning takes place in a variety of ways – through text, audio, video and computer. Television and radio are not normally used.

Distance learning is usually provided by employers to meet an identified learning need in their employees. The learning can be compulsory or voluntary.

- **Active learning**
Active learning is something quite different. It is learning by doing, and is designed to teach employees specific in-company procedures or skills. You can learn, for example, how to fill in certain forms or carry out ordering procedures. You can learn about products or services.

The idea here is to provide newcomers to the work situation with a means of learning which is standard throughout the company, where employees can learn at their own pace and managers do not have to spend a lot of time training new staff.

Procedures, systems and skills learnt in this way are definitely skills and knowledge that an employee will need to do the job. Again a variety of methods is used (text, audio, video and computer). Short tests are built into the programme at intervals so that employees have to prove their ability to master one stage before moving on to the next. Learning how to work a keyboard or a particular computer package is a very good example of active learning – or self-teach, as it is sometimes called.

Here the costs are paid entirely by the employer, and the employee learns during working hours.

Active learning is used to learn specific skills, knowledge and procedures needed to do a job. It has to be learnt by all employees who need to know it.

126

Self-study checklist for open and distance learning

- Take up any good self-study opportunity offered to you
- Plan definite study times
- Make sure you have adequate facilities: eg peace and quiet to learn, equipment, facilities for playing tapes, videos etc as necessary. Courses will always tell you what you need to complete the course
- Organise understanding and support from your family and/or your work colleagues
- Don't have long gaps between sections or stages: it is difficult to re-start once you have stopped
- Get projects, essays, assignments etc in on time
- Make good use of tutor or trainer support, and don't be afraid to ask for help
- Attend any residential weekends or sessions which are part of the course. It is a great opportunity to talk to other people in the same boat
- Persevere. It's hard work, but worth it in the end.

Training courses

Many employees are sent on training courses from time to time. These courses take place off the job (in a place different from your actual work position), sometimes on company premises, sometimes in hotels, sometimes in colleges or training centres. The course will be led by a tutor or trainer, who is totally responsible for everything that happens on the course.

Many people are apprehensive about attending courses, because they think they will be asked to do things they do not know how to do, and generally make fools of themselves. This very rarely happens, and all professional trainers will understand how you feel and ease you in gently.

Sometimes you are sent on a course because you have asked for this training at your Appraisal. Sometimes you are sent because everyone at that level is sent anyway. It is unusual for people to be sent on courses which are totally unsuitable for them, but it can happen sometimes.

A training course usually lasts two or more days, and a seminar tends to last for one day, although there is no hard and fast rule about this. A workshop is normally one or two days long and requires you to participate almost all the time. Courses are usually a mixture of 'input' (lecture) by the trainer and participation by the course members; at a seminar there will be a lot of input from the trainer, speaker or presenter and a small amount of participation.

To get the best out of a training course:
- Prepare
- Participate
- Practise

● Prepare

Make sure you know why you are going on the course and what you want to get out of it. Read the joining instructions (the papers which tell you what it is about, where it is etc) carefully and any course brochure you are sent.

Talk to your manager about the course and agree with her or him what specifically you want to get out of it. Ask yourself what you would like to be able to do or know at the end of the course which you did not do or know at the beginning.

If you have been asked to read or write certain things, do this as thoroughly as you can. Lack of preparation will show up on the course.

Check whether facilities include such things as a swimming pool, squash court etc so that you can take the right equipment. Arrive on time so that you are ready to take part in the first activity, whether it is a training session or a meal.

● Participate

You will get out of the course as much as you put into it. Ask questions; challenge the trainer or the other course members; work with enthusiasm. If you arrive in a negative frame of mind you will take time to become positive and will have missed what was good during the first part of the course. Even if you think you know all there is to know about a subject, there is usually something more you can learn; sometimes it is just helpful to confirm that you are doing the right thing. Do not underestimate the value that your experience could be to other, less experienced, people on the course; a good trainer will recognise this and use it to advantage.

If the course uses special equipment, such as video, make sure you get your turn. It might terrify you, appearing in front of the camera, but it will help you learn; you will enjoy it once you have done it and will want to do it again.

Participate in the non-work activities too. There is no reason why training courses should not be fun. If it is a residential course you will often find there is evening work, but it is usually sandwiched between dinner and meeting in the bar. It does not matter if you are up until the early hours of the morning working or socialising, provided you are fit to participate to the full the next morning.

Towards the end of a course you are often asked to make an Action Plan for yourself. You might feel embarrassed at having to do this, but a course is no good unless you carry what you have learnt back to your everyday work, and an Action Plan helps you to do this.

You will also often be asked to give your opinion of the course on an Evaluation Form. Take time to do this. The trainer will want to know what was good and what was bad about the course so that it can be altered as necessary. Hotel rooms often have guest questionnaires, too. Fill these in if you can. How can anyone improve if they are not told what is wrong? Remember to give praise where due – make the positive comments as well as the negative ones (see Chapter 8).

- **Practise**

When you get back to work, do not shove your course papers in a drawer and forget about them. Talk to your manager about the course, if s/he has not asked you about it first, and mention your Action Plan, so that you can get help with it, if necessary. Set yourself a target of about three months when you can look back and see how much you have improved. You will often find you have done more than you thought you had. It is very good for the morale!

Training course checklist

- Read the Joining Instructions and take any action you are asked to do
- Discuss the course with your manager, and decide what you want to get out of it
- Participate as much as possible in the work and the socialising
- Plan what you are going to do after the course
- Discuss your plan with your manager, and put it into action

 Work experience

If you are at school or college you will probably get a chance to go on work experience. This is a very good opportunity to get to know what working in the world of business is like. You will come across different types of bosses and working methods, and might be able to decide you like working in one type of business rather than another.

If you find you do like working for a particular company, you will be able to see the sort of person they have working for them, and the type of person they are looking for. You can find out more about the company, discover whether there are any vacancies, and prepare yourself for an interview.

Work experience is also the place where you can get practical experience in a real working environment of the things you have been learning at school or college. Sometimes you have to be a bit pushy to get as much out of it as possible. Work experience can last as little as two weeks or even an odd day here and there, so it really is important to learn as much as you can.

Work experience is often organised by a teacher or lecturer who is not your own tutor. This means that you have to work through your tutor to get the experience you need. Agree with your tutor **exactly** what you want to do on work experience, so that your needs can be passed on to the person organising the work experience. You will not necessarily get all you want, but you will stand some chance of getting some of it; try to make sure you get the experience you need to achieve the Performance Criteria for the Units or Elements in your scheme of work (see Assessments at the beginning of this chapter).

Take your checklist with you when you start your work experience, and try to get your temporary boss to agree to let you do what is on the list. You might have to explain what certain things mean, because business people are not necessarily familiar with Units, Elements and Performance Criteria, but if you understand what you are doing you are more likely to be able to get other people to understand as well (see Assessments again).

Be a good employee, even if the work is boring and not to your taste. Your employer has had to make special arrangements to take you on and you will make it difficult for work experience in the future if you do not pull your weight, or if you grumble. You need to be a bit pushy sometimes, as we said at the beginning of this section, but do not go over the top and make life difficult for yourself and others who may follow. Get your head down and get on with the work – it is only for a short time.

If you have Units or Elements to get signed off (see Assessments), get this done before you leave the work experience placement. It is very difficult and time-consuming to have to go back, perhaps months later, to get a signature. In many cases your Assessor will not be able to credit you with that Element or Unit unless you have the signature.

Thank your temporary employer for having you there and letting you learn. If people have been particularly helpful, tell the company so and feed this information back to your college or school. It is useful to know who are the good work experience providers.

Work experience checklist

- Agree with your tutor, teacher or lecturer what you want to achieve

- Make sure your temporary employer understands what you need to do
- Be a good employee
- Get achievement signed off
- Thank your employer and feed comments back to your school or college

---

Practice

The next time you take up any one of the self-development opportunities mentioned in this chapter:
- Appraisal
- Assessment
- Self-study
- Training course
- Work experience

make a definite effort to read through the section, work through the checklist and analyse, after the event, whether you did, in fact, get the best out of the opportunity.

Points to remember from this chapter

- Prepare for each opportunity as it comes your way
- Plan what you want to do or say
- Participate fully
- Practise what you have learnt

11 Quality Service

In this chapter:
- What is quality service?
- Service chains
- Sympathy and empathy
- What more 'could' you do?

 ## What is quality service?

What do you remember when you go into a shop, a garage or a restaurant? If the service was adequate you probably will not remember anything in particular.

If you got poor service you will remember it and tell your friends 'I went into so-and-so, and they ignored me completely – and then when I asked for the thing I'd ordered, they said it hadn't come in. I shan't go there again'. Your friends will remember what you said and the next time they think of going to so-and-so they will have a little doubt in their minds, and perhaps go elsewhere.

If you get really excellent service, you will remember that too. You are not quite so likely to tell your friends, because people prefer to grumble rather than to praise (see Chapter 8 – recognition and encouragement). However, you might remember to say 'You know that whatever-it-is I ordered from so-and-so? They rang to let me know it wasn't in yet – saved me going in to get it. Said they'd let me know when it comes in'. Your friends will remember what you said, and subconsciously will think they might go to that place next time.

Whenever you think or learn about service you will consider fulfilling the customer's needs, whether that customer is external or internal to your company. Real **quality** service is fulfilling these needs, whatever they are, **and** giving that little bit extra – the bit that is not in the book.

You cannot say exactly what quality service is, because it will be different on every occasion. It will depend on the customer, the customer's needs, your ability to fulfil those needs **and** to give that little bit extra.

131

Service chains

The basis of all service is to fulfil the customer's needs. It sounds simple, but can be quite complicated, because very many people are involved in making sure the customers get what they want.

We will consider a service 'chain', and see how many people are involved. We will then think about what can go wrong at each stage, because a chain is only as strong as its weakest link.

The retail service chain

1 Customer goes into electrical store and orders new fridge/freezer, to be delivered
↓

2 Sales assistant keys details into computer, checks the model is in stock, arranges delivery date and takes payment by credit card
↓

3 Customer details are collected overnight via the telephone line by the central storage depot clerk
↓

4 Storage depot data processing operator feeds details on to 'picking note' (the document which tells the fork lift truck driver what is wanted and where to find it in the depot)
↓

5 Fork lift truck driver finds fridge/freezer and takes it on truck to despatch area of depot
↓

6 Loader loads fridge/freezer on to company's vehicle
↓

7 Central storage depot driver delivers fridge/freezer to local storage depot
↓

8 Local driver picks up fridge/freezer, loads it onto van and delivers it to customer
↓

9 Meanwhile accounts office has been processing credit card payment.

How many people are involved in this chain, not counting the customer? There are at least eight people involved:
- Sales assistant
- Central storage depot clerk

- Storage depot data processing operator
- Fork lift truck driver
- Loader
- Central storage depot driver
- Local van driver
- Accounts clerk

There is also the buyer, who bought the fridge/freezer for the company to sell, the marketing executive who designed the advertising material, the clerk who authorised the credit card payment, the shop manager, the shop cleaner, the person who looks after the company's vehicles and so on. There are a tremendous number of people involved in one transaction, and a lot of times when things could go wrong.

Exercise 1

For each link in the retail chain, from link number 2 onwards, here is one example of what could go wrong. Think about the example and, with your neighbour, decide what the consequences of that mistake could be:

Chain link No 2 – Sales assistant takes details
Sales assistant gets customer's address slightly wrong and puts down No 21 instead of No 12. What are the consequences?

Chain link No 3 – Central storage depot clerk collects computer details overnight
The last person in the shop forgets to set the computer for overnight 'polling', so no details are collected. What are the consequences?

Chain link No 4 – DP operator feeds details into picking note
DP operator feeds in wrong fridge/freezer number, ordering the wrong fridge/freezer. What are the consequences?

Chain link No 5 – Fork lift truck driver picks fridge/freezer and takes it to despatch area
Driver is careless, and knocks fridge/freezer while driving truck around depot. What are the consequences?

Chain link No 6 – Loader loads fridge/freezer on to delivery vehicle
Loader loads fridge/freezer on to wrong vehicle – one which is going to another part of the country. What are the consequences?

134

> **Chain link No 7 – Central depot driver delivers fridge/freezer to local depot**
> Central driver is late for work, and misses the connection with the local van going out. What are the consequences?
>
> **Chain link No 8 – Local driver delivers fridge/freezer**
> Driver delivers in the afternoon, when a morning delivery was promised. What are the consequences?
>
> **Chain link No 9 – Accounts clerk processes credit card payment**
> Clerk is very behind with processing the credit card payments, so they go off to the credit card company several weeks later. What are the consequences?

It is unlikely that all these things would go wrong for one fridge/freezer, but quite possible that **one** link in the chain could break.

Check your answers for each link in the retail chain against these ideas:

Link No 2 – Wrong house number
The driver calls at No 21. Nobody at home. Frustrated driver. Returns fridge/freezer to local depot. Frustrated customer. Second delivery has to be made. Costs company money and goodwill.

Link No 3 – Computer details not collected overnight
Shop misses allotted 'window' of computer time. Details are delayed 24 hours. Fridge/freezer not delivered to local depot. Local driver does not have goods to deliver and does not call at No 12. Frustrated customer.

Link No 4 – Wrong item picked
Wrong fridge/freezer is delivered. Frustrated customer. Fridge/freezer has to be returned to central depot and replaced with right model. Costs company money and goodwill.

Link No 5 – Careless driver damages fridge/freezer
Customer unpacks delivery, discovers damage, has to 'phone and arrange replacement. Frustrated customer. Fridge/freezer has to be collected from address and new one delivered. Costs company money and goodwill.

Link No 6 – Goods loaded on to wrong vehicle
Fridge/freezer ends up in wrong depot. They have to 'phone to find

out what to do with it. Local driver in right depot has nothing to deliver. Nothing arrives at address. Frustrated customer. Costs company money and goodwill.

Link No 7 – Fridge/freezer not delivered to local depot
Local driver has nothing to deliver. Does not call at No 12. Frustrated customer. Driver has to go out specially. Costs company money and goodwill.

Link No 8 – Driver delivers at wrong time of day
Customer has gone back to work. Nobody is at No 12. Arrangements have to be made all over again. Frustrated customer. Costs company money and goodwill.

Link No 9 – Accounts clerk behind with work
Company does not get money from credit card company. Customer is happy – fridge/freezer has been delivered. Credit card company is happy – it does not have to pay electrical company. Electrical company is **not** happy! Does not get its money promptly and cannot bank it.

You can see how easily one small mistake by one person in the chain can lead to a frustrated customer and the company losing money and goodwill. It is very important that everyone in the chain does their work accurately and promptly – and that is only for normal service.

In a normal service situation the customer gets the right goods at the right time and the company is paid its money promptly. What about quality service – giving that little bit extra?

Here are some examples of what various people in the chain could have done to make good service into excellent service. Note that these are things people **could** have done, not what they **should** have done. For example, the sales assistant **should** have checked the customer's address details; the sales assistant **could** also have asked whether the customer's house was easy to find, and passed any additional information on so that the driver did not waste time looking for the house. That would have been giving quality service to an internal colleague, so that the external customer also gets quality service. Here are some more examples:

- The truck driver who knocked the fridge/freezer in the central depot could have checked for damage before the goods left the depot.
- The central delivery driver could have 'phoned to say the delivery to the local depot would be late; the local driver could have waited a few minutes.
- When the local delivery driver missed the morning delivery, the office

could have 'phoned the customer to say what was happening. Perhaps the customer could have contacted a work colleague and stayed at home for an extra hour.

- The accounts clerk could have let someone know that work was well behind, and asked for help. Alternatively, and better still, a colleague could have noticed that the clerk was snowed under and **offered** help.

Top quality service is all about giving that bit extra, putting yourself in the customer's shoes, going the extra mile – whichever expression you like to use. It is about empathising with the customer – not only sympathising, but empathising.

 ## Sympathy and empathy

It is very easy to sympathise with someone – that is, to feel sorry for them, if something has gone wrong, and to say how much you sympathise. Sympathy and understanding are very valuable, because they show someone that you are able to put yourself in their shoes and that they are not alone in their difficulty. Empathy goes a step further. Empathy means that you not only sympathise, but do something or help the person to do something to get them out of their difficulty. Here is a story to illustrate true empathy:

Once upon a time there was a donkey, which belonged to a village. Everyone in the village loved the donkey; the men admired its strength and willingness; the women fed it and looked after it and the children played with it.

One day – disaster! The donkey went missing. Nobody could find it anywhere, even though a huge search party was mounted. Everybody was really upset; the children cried because they had lost their friend, the women missed the donkey's warm good nature and the men had to work without their trusted helper.

After a while, one of the old men of the village thought 'Now, if I were the donkey, where would I go?' He really put himself in the donkey's shoes, thinking the donkey's thoughts and sympathising with it. And the old man went to a field where nobody had thought to look – and lo and behold, there was the donkey.

The old man had shown real sympathy, but if he had stopped there, he would have stayed in the field, lost with the donkey. Now he did something a little extra, and with carrots and kind words he persuaded the donkey to come back to the village with him, showing empathy with the donkey's needs.

So the old man and the donkey returned to the village, and everyone lived happily ever after!

Exercise 2

Here are some examples of people with difficulties. It would be easy to sympathise with them, but what could you do to show real empathy, and to help them out of their difficulty?

1 Your friend at work has just spilled coffee all over the papers s/he was working on. What can you do?

2 You are a receptionist. A visitor has just 'phoned to say he thinks he left a file on your reception desk when he visited earlier that day. What can you do?

3 Your boss has not arrived for a meeting. You have heard there has been an accident and the traffic is held up – you think your boss has probably got stuck in the traffic. What can you do?

4 You work in a small supermarket. A customer cannot read the price tickets, because he has forgotten his spectacles, and asks you to tell him what the price of a certain item is. What can you do?

In each case the first thing to be done is obvious, but what extra can you do to show empathy, that is, to help the person out of the difficulty? Check your ideas with these:

- **The coffee spill**
  Sympathy: say how sorry you are – help to clear up the mess
  Empathy: offer to help re-do the papers, or get another set of copies, whatever is necessary

- **The lost file**
  Sympathy: say how awkward it must be – look for the file at reception
  Empathy: ask where else the visitor might have left the file – offer to ring the offices the visitor has been in

- **The late arrival**
  Sympathy: when you realise your boss is going to be late, contact the meeting to let them know

138

Empathy: make sure all the papers are ready to hand to your boss immediately s/he walks through the door – be at the door when your boss comes in – take your boss's coat, briefcase etc (anything not needed for the meeting)

- **The forgotten spectacles**
  Sympathy: read the price and hand the customer the item
  Empathy: ask if there are any other items he wants in that section – warn other members of staff who are in the other sectors to look out for the customer and give him help if needed.

What more 'could' you do?

In the previous section you were thinking about helping people out of difficulties. In the final section of this chapter, think about good service that you give and how you can turn it into top quality service – the sort of service that your customers, both internal and external, will really appreciate and remember.

Exercise 3

You have done everything you 'should' do; now think about what else you 'could' do? Here are some examples:

1 A customer has written to say they have moved house and would you note their change of address. You have altered the address on the computer list and everywhere else you can think of. What more could you do?

2 Someone junior to you is carrying a lot of heavy boxes, and you open the door for him so he can go out easily. What more could you do?

3 You have to serve tea or coffee to regular visitors as part of your job. You have asked whether they want it black, white, with sugar etc and made sure it is served as they want it. What more could you do?

- In the first situation you could tell the others whose work is to do with that customer whose address has changed – just in case they keep their own address lists. If it is a really good customer, you send a 'welcome to your new home' card.

- In the second situation you could check if there are any more doors along the immediate route and offer to help open the doors and/or carry the boxes.
- In the third situation you could make a note of how they take their coffee or tea and make sure they get good service next time they visit. Do not assume that they still want their coffee black, no sugar – they might have changed their tastes. When offering the coffee or tea, say something like 'Black, no sugar, Mr Robinson?', giving him a chance to change his mind. Your forethought will be much appreciated.

Quality service is not something you can pin down and say 'that's it'. It is a feeling that you have been treated really well, whether you are an internal or an external customer.

Points to remember from this chapter

- Top quality service is remembered
- A service chain is only as strong as its weakest link
- Simple mistakes can have disastrous consequences
- Empathy goes further than sympathy
- What extra 'could' you do when you have done all you 'should' do?

12 Creative Thinking

In this chapter:
- How creative are you?
- Barriers to creative thinking
- Techniques
- Getting things done

When you start a new job it takes time to learn the procedures, systems, skills and conventions; it takes time, too, to get to know the people and build the business relationships. You cannot sweep in like a ferocious new broom and alter everything at once. This is true even when you have some experience and have been given the job of creating a new department or section.

However, once you are settled in the job it is very easy to get sucked into routines and ways of thinking which are not very productive. New ideas should be welcomed, even if they cannot always be used, and many companies do welcome creative thoughts which lead to improvements in working practices.

This chapter is about ways in which you can use your own creative thinking to make suggestions about better ways of doing things without seeming too pushy or alienating others.

 ## How creative are you?

How good is your lateral thinking? How good are you at thinking beyond the obvious and seeing solutions which are imaginative?

Exercise 1
Here are four problems. See how good you are at solving them.

- *Problem No 1*

```
.  .  .

.  .  .

.  .  .
```

Join all 9 dots using only four straight lines going to each dot only once and not taking your pen or pencil off the paper.

- *Problem No 2*
Give the next three letters in this sequence.

OTTFFSS

- *Problem No 3*
Draw this circle with a dot in the centre without taking your pen or pencil off the paper.

- *Problem No 4*
Add one line to make this six.

IX

142

Here are solutions to the problem; there may be others equally sensible.

- *Problem No 1*

The trick here is to go **outside** the square of dots. You can start at any of the corner dots; use these instructions to succeed in doing it in one way.

1   2   3

4   5   6

7   8   9

Start at dot no 7 and draw diagonally through 5 to 3.

Draw from 3 though 6 to 9 and down beyond 9.

Draw back up through 8 and 4 and again out beyond the dots.

Draw back through dot 1 to dot 2, and the problem is solved.

People often get stuck in the 9 dots because the dots are in the form of a square and they think they must not go outside the dots.
Message: think beyond barriers which seem to be there but which are not in fact there.

- *Problem No 2*

The answer is ENT.

   The lateral thinking takes you away from letters and makes you think about figures. Start thinking figures, and you will see that the first letter of **O**ne, **T**wo, **T**hree, **F**our, **F**ive, **S**ix and **S**even give the original sequence. Add **E**ight, **N**ine and **T**en and you have the solution.

Message: don't take things at face value. Think round the subject or think opposites and let your mind open itself out to other possibilities.

- *Problem No 3*

This seems almost impossible until you start thinking in 3-D. Fold over a corner of a piece of paper and start your drawing on the back. Draw the dot in the middle on the point of the folded corner **and** on the front of your sheet of paper.

Next, without lifting your pen or pencil draw a line from the dot on the back of the paper out towards the fold and then round to the edge of the folded bit and onto the front of the piece of paper.

Finally, let the fold go and join up the circle on the front of the paper.

Message: there are often more angles or sides to a problem than you can see immediately. Let your mind become 3-D and think about things from different points of view.

- *Problem No 3*

SIX

To make this into six by adding one line, add an S on to the beginning: **S**IX. Nobody said it had to be a straight line!

Message: again, don't go for the obvious, and don't put words into people's mouths that they do not say. Don't assume!

The purpose of trying to solve those problems was not only to see how good you are at thinking round and through a problem, but to show you how easy it is to get into a rut of thought patterns and to see barriers which do not exist.

 ## Barriers to creative thinking

At school we get praised for being clever, logical, good at maths, science and languages. Children who are good at art and creative subjects tend to be thought of as dreamers.

The result of this is that the people who are not 'naturally' creative do not give that part of their brain enough exercise, and get out of the habit of thinking and acting in a creative and imaginative sort of way.

It is important in some circumstances to do exactly what we are told to do, and stick rigidly to set procedures. For example, where safety is concerned you must obey the rules.

It is not sensible, either, to become a complete rebel and upset things for everyone around you, but a little creative thinking can often solve a problem by looking at it from a different angle, or ignoring those imaginary barriers.

The sorts of barriers you might find at work are:
1 Things are done this way because they always have been.
2 People in lower or middle management put a stop on new ideas.
3 There is an 'us and them' division, and you must belong to 'us'.
  'Them' could be Head Office, management, other departments, other sections or almost any other part of the organisation.
4 The atmosphere is negative rather than positive (see Chapter 8).
What can you do to overcome these barriers without rocking the boat?

● *Barrier No 1: 'It's always been done like that'*
'It' was probably done like that in the first place for a good reason. You need to acknowledge that fact and resist being scornful about how something is done.

If you can see a better way of doing something, suggest that circumstances have changed, and it might be helpful to everyone to re-think the way that something is done. You need to be aware, also, that you in your position cannot necessarily see the whole picture, and what might seem a good idea from your point of view would make life difficult in another part of the company or organisation.

Do not let the barriers put you off; recognise those that are real and try to 'ignore' those that are imaginary.

- *Barrier No 2: People who stop ideas*

This is quite difficult to handle, particularly if you are full of ideas which keep getting squashed. You can feel very frustrated and be tempted to give up trying.

People at junior or middle management level sometimes do put stoppers on ideas put forward by junior members of staff, but they do not all do it for the same reason. Some people are just too busy to listen to other people's ideas; some do not feel secure enough in their own positions to allow new ideas to touch them; some genuinely try to protect junior members of staff from being over-enthusiastic; some unfortunately put forward the ideas as their own, and do not acknowledge where they came from.

What can you do if you have good ideas which you are convinced will work, and find this barrier above you? You can sometimes go round the barrier by using the staff suggestion scheme or other means of communicating up the line. Most well-run companies have some method of tapping into the ideas of their employees; they may be meetings or quality circles or total quality management teams or something along those lines. If so, watch out for them and join them.

Sometimes you can go over the barrier to the person above the 'stopper'. It depends very much on personalities and the atmosphere in which you all work. You would have to judge the situation as it arises, but an appraisal system might let you do this (see Chapter 10).

Occasionally you can begin to put your ideas into practice yourself and quietly get things done without upsetting anybody. For example, an improved filing system (paper or electronic) can be introduced bit by bit until the whole system has been re-done.

It is unlikely that you will be working for the same people in junior or middle management for a very long time without some staff movement being made. If you find your ideas have been totally stopped, keep them for the future. The opportunity often comes sooner than you think.

- *Barrier No 3: Us and them*

It is unusual to find a company or organisation without some sort of 'us and them' atmosphere. This is sad, because everyone in the company is working towards the same goals, or should be.

'Us and them' shows itself by people grumbling about other parts of the company, or people, or levels of management. It is the opposite of thinking of the other people in the company as your internal customers (see Chapter 1). Instead of trying to anticipate people's needs and doing their best to meet those needs and exceed them, individuals or sometimes whole departments go out of their way to be less than helpful and sometimes really obstructive.

146

It takes a lot of courage to go against your section or workmates and to work with people who are 'them' instead of against them. Many junior members of staff do not have that courage or that confidence, which is understandable. If you find yourself in this position, you might choose to keep a low profile and get on with your work. You might feel you can do something positive to break down the 'us and them' barrier, simply by making contact with 'them' and finding out what they do and what they need from you. If you cannot do that, at least you can stop yourself joining in the grumbling and try to work with 'them' as far as possible.

- *Barrier No 4: The negative atmosphere*

This is very like Barrier No 3, except that the negative atmosphere is general, and often directed at the whole company or organisation rather than at one part of it.

If an atmosphere is very negative and morale is generally low, it is very difficult to do your work well and enjoy it, and almost impossible to be creative and put forward new ideas or overcome problems.

What can you do in this situation? You can only try to ignore the atmosphere, do your own work as well as you can and look for opportunities to get out of the environment. This does not necessarily mean changing jobs, or asking for a transfer, although this could be an option. It might mean keeping an eye open for special projects or chances of further education or training which you could undertake. Look beyond the immediate unhealthy atmosphere and try to do something positive yourself, so that when the opportunity for better things arrives, you are ready to take it.

Sometimes the only barrier to creative thinking is yourself, because you are prepared to accept things as they are, even if you are unhappy about the situation or the problem. There is usually something to be done about everything.

Techniques

If you have a problem to solve and are stuck, there are various techniques you can use to try a little creative thinking and see different ways round the problem.

● Brainstorming

This is one of the most useful techniques. It can open your mind to all sorts of ideas; you generally do this with other people.

The basis of brainstorming is to throw as many ideas into the pool as possible, not worrying whether the ideas are sensible, stupid, possible, practicable or outrageous. Take a problem or a subject and write down, as a group, anything that comes into your head about the topic. Do it as fast as you can, without giving too much thought to it – you are looking for quantity, not quality at this stage. For example, if your subject is 'What to do with a fork', you might write up on the board; eat, dig, pin something down, bend it, clean it, wash it up, garden, plant, use it as a catapult, stab, etc.

One idea often leads to another. There are some rules to brainstorming, which helps the ideas to flow freely, which are:

- Anything goes – even the wildest ideas
- Write **every** idea down
- Repetition does not matter
- Accept all ideas
- Do not be judgemental about ideas, verbally or by body language
- Keep going as long as you can and as fast as you can

Exercise 2

With your group, brainstorm the following topic. Ask someone to write all the ideas on a board, and remember to obey the rules.

Topic: 'What you can do with a paper clip'

Brainstorming is a very good technique for solving problems. Do not struggle with them on your own. Have a couple of minutes' brainstorm with your colleagues, and you will be surprised what ideas will emerge. Once you have got them all down, cross out the ones which are impossible (but be sure they **are** impossible) and consider all the others.

Some years ago in the United States, a group of people was trying to solve the problem of preventing theft and burglary from houses. They had a brainstorm, in which one of the ideas was 'We should all become policemen'; this seemed an impossible idea, but from that thought the 'Neighbourhood Watch Scheme' was born. Practical solutions can come from the most unlikely ideas.

● Breaking routine

This is another good way of coming up with fresh ideas, particularly if you are writing, and are stuck for ideas about what to write. Break your

148

routine, and do something different – it gives you a fresh outlook on life.
Here are some ideas:

- Get up earlier
- Get up later
- Have something different for breakfast
- Have breakfast
- Go to work a different way
- Stop for a break at a different time
- Go out to lunch
- Stay in for lunch
- Change the angle of your chair
- Rearrange your desk

Do something different, and get a different perspective on life.

- **Random thinking**

Random thinking means picking a word, a phrase, a happening or an
object at random, thinking about it and then relating it to your problem
or the situation in which you are stuck.

For example, open a book and pick a word at random, or go out into
the street or the countryside and look up to see something, anything,
which catches your eye. The word could be 'cold'; the object could be a
roof. How could you relate those words to your problem or situation?

Suppose the problem is 'getting hold of someone on the telephone
and they are not there'. How can 'cold' or 'roof' help you? Any ideas?
'Cold' might make you think of early mornings, so you try ringing even
earlier; it might make you think of ice, which leads to food or drink, so
you could try ringing at lunchtime, or go to see the person in the pub.
'Roof' might make you think of slates; slates could lead to writing, which
could lead you round to sending a fax instead.

Does this sound far-fetched? Perhaps, but it is a way of starting a
chain of word associations, which opens your mind to let the ideas flow
in.

- **Making a list**

This technique is useful when you have a difficult decision to make. It is
not the same as brainstorming, because here you are working on your
own and writing down all the possible solutions to your problem. Write
down every possibility, even the remotest ones – think the unthinkable;
include things which are possible but which you know you will never
do. Making the list makes you see the problem from all sorts of different
angles, some of which may have been lurking at the back of your mind;
writing them down brings them to the forefront. It is similar to the
technique you used in Chapter 4 when you were thinking about
unfulfilled expectations at work.

When you have finished the list, and not before, start crossing off the options which are not possible. You probably knew they were not possible as you wrote them down, but the act of writing them down and crossing them off helps you put them right out of the running. Gradually cross out all the options you are not prepared to take until you are left with two, or three at the most. You have whittled down the choices and can make your decision by weighing up one against the other – your mind is focused on those choices alone. You might in the end take the decision which you thought you would take anyway, but this technique has made you consider all the options, so that you are happy, or as happy as you can be, about the decision you have made.

For example, you might be offered promotion which means moving to another part of the country. If you stay where you are you will miss a good opportunity for promotion and more money: if you move it might mean leaving behind family, friends, interests, responsibilities and so on. You might make a list of the options like this:

- Take the job and move permanently
- Refuse the job and stay put
- Commute daily
- Work away during the week and come home at weekends
- Refuse the job, but explain why and ask to be considered for something nearer home
- Take the job, move house and take your family with you

The first two were probably the first to spring to mind, but with a bit of creative thinking other possibilities emerge. Commuting might be unthinkable, because of distance, but you have made a decision to reject that option and your mind gets used to thinking round a subject and taking decisions.

Making the final decision can be tough, but you will have clarified your mind and made sure that you are thinking clearly about the pros and cons of the decision you have to make. You might even surprise yourself, and come up with something you would never have considered if you had not done some creative thinking.

Do not let the creative side of your brain go to sleep. Use it. Everyone has good ideas at some time, so give yourself a chance and let your mind be open to all sorts of ideas from all sorts of directions. Think – creatively.

Getting things done

Practice

1 Think of a problem you have to solve, or a decision you have to make. It could be a minor problem or decision, like what to wear for a special occasion. It could be a major problem, or decision, like what your next career move will be.

Choose one of the techniques you have just been reading about, or a combination of two of them, and use it or them to help you solve your problem. For example, you could do some brainstorming on what to wear by asking other people who may also be involved in the special occasion, and then make a list to help you decide. You could break your routine, do something different and walk to work while you are thinking about a career move, and then make the list to help you decide the next step to take.

These are only examples. Choose a problem or a decision that you have now and set to work to get something done about it.

2 Once you have decided what to do, make a list of the steps you have to take to carry your decision through. It might be collecting more information, it might be asking advice, it might be trying something out – it could be almost anything.

3 Take the first step, which is often the hardest. Once you have taken it, you are well on your way to getting something done.

Points to remember from this chapter

- Don't be put off by barriers which do not exist
- Don't take things at face value
- Look at things from different angles
- Think beyond the obvious
- Be your own person, and do not be discouraged by other people's negativity
- Use a definite technique to help you make decisions or solve problems
- There is usually something to be done about everything

People are so interesting. Do some people watching and practise your people skills wherever you are. It takes the tedium out of life and makes sure you are the type of people person others want to be and work with.

☐ Index